PANDAS FOR FINANCE

Power Precision

Hayden Van Der Post

Reactive Publishing

CONTENTS

CHAPTER 1: INTRODUCTION TO PANDAS AND FINANCE

The Pandas library is a cornerstone of data analysis in Python, renowned for its powerful, flexible, and high-performance data manipulation capabilities. Initially developed by Wes McKinney in 2008, Pandas has grown into one of the most popular libraries among data scientists, analysts, and financial professionals. Its versatility spans various domains, but its prowess in handling time-series data, data frames, and advanced indexing makes it particularly indispensable for finance.

Pandas emerged from the need to analyze large volumes of financial data efficiently. Wes McKinney, working at AQR Capital Management, saw the potential of having a robust data manipulation tool that could seamlessly handle time-series data and complex financial datasets. Over the years, Pandas has evolved, integrating more functionalities and optimizations, driven by contributions from the open-source community and commercial entities alike. Today, it stands as a testament to collaborative development, continuously improving and expanding its capabilities.

Core Concepts and Data Structures

In Pandas there are its two primary data structures: Series and DataFrame.

- Series: A one-dimensional labeled array capable of holding any data type. It is akin to a column in a spreadsheet, with labels known as the index. Series is highly efficient for time series data, allowing easy manipulation and access.

- DataFrame: A two-dimensional labeled data structure with columns of potentially different types. Think of it as a table or spreadsheet with rows and columns. DataFrames are the most commonly used data structures in Pandas, offering a vast array of functionalities for data manipulation, cleaning, and analysis.

These core structures facilitate complex operations on large datasets, making Pandas an essential tool for financial analytics.

Key Features and Functionalities

Pandas' strength lies in its ability to effortlessly handle and manipulate data. Here are some of the key features that make Pandas indispensable:

1. Data Alignment and Indexing: Pandas provides powerful tools for aligning data based on labels, which is crucial when dealing with time-series data or merging datasets from

different sources.

2. Handling Missing Data: Financial datasets often contain missing values. Pandas offers a range of methods to handle these, from simple imputation techniques to more sophisticated interpolation methods.

3. GroupBy Functionality: Grouping data based on certain criteria and performing aggregate functions is a breeze with Pandas. This is incredibly useful for financial analytics, such as calculating average returns by sector or summing up trading volumes by date.

4. Time Series Analysis: Pandas excels in handling time series data, offering functionalities like resampling, rolling window calculations, and time-based indexing. This is particularly beneficial for financial professionals dealing with stock prices, trading volumes, or economic indicators.

5. Data Cleaning and Preparation: Pandas simplifies the often tedious process of data cleaning. It provides functions for removing duplicates, transforming data types, normalizing data, and more.

6. Integration with Other Libraries: Pandas seamlessly integrates with other Python libraries like NumPy, SciPy, Matplotlib, and Scikit-Learn. This interoperability enhances its capabilities, allowing for more comprehensive data analysis and machine learning workflows.

Practical Applications in Finance

Pandas is not just a theoretical tool; its real-world applications in finance are vast and varied. Here are some practical scenarios where Pandas proves invaluable:

- Stock Price Analysis: Importing historical stock price data, calculating moving averages, and identifying trends.
- Portfolio Management: Analyzing and optimizing investment portfolios based on historical returns and risk metrics.
- Risk Management: Calculating Value-at-Risk (VaR), stress testing portfolios, and performing scenario analysis.
- Economic Data Analysis: Handling large economic datasets, performing time series analysis, and visualizing trends.

Example: Simple Stock Analysis with Pandas

Let's delve into a practical example to illustrate the power of Pandas. We'll perform a simple stock price analysis by importing historical data, calculating moving averages, and visualizing the trends.

```python
import pandas as pd
import matplotlib.pyplot as plt

# Importing historical stock price data
data = pd.read_csv('historical_stock_prices.csv', parse_dates=['Date'], index_col='Date')

# Calculating moving averages
data['20_day_MA'] = data['Close'].rolling(window=20).mean()
data['50_day_MA'] = data['Close'].rolling(window=50).mean()
```

```
# Plotting the stock prices and moving averages
plt.figure(figsize=(12, 6))
plt.plot(data['Close'], label='Close Price')
plt.plot(data['20_day_MA'], label='20 Day Moving Average')
plt.plot(data['50_day_MA'], label='50 Day Moving Average')
plt.title('Stock Price and Moving Averages')
plt.xlabel('Date')
plt.ylabel('Price')
plt.legend()
plt.show()
```

In this example, we first import the necessary libraries and read the historical stock price data into a DataFrame. We then calculate the 20-day and 50-day moving averages of the closing prices. Finally, we plot the closing prices and the moving averages to visualize the trends. This demonstrates how Pandas can simplify complex data manipulation tasks and provide valuable insights with minimal code.

The Pandas library is undeniably a powerful tool for financial data analysis. Its robust data structures, comprehensive functionalities, and ease of use make it an essential asset for finance professionals. Whether you're managing portfolios, analyzing stock prices, or handling large economic datasets, Pandas equips you with the tools to perform sophisticated analyses efficiently. As we move forward in this book, you'll discover how to leverage Pandas to its fullest potential, transforming your financial data analysis capabilities.

2. Importance of Pandas in Financial Data Analysis

In the intricate world of finance, data is the currency of decision-making. The ability to dissect, analyze, and interpret financial data can spell the difference between success and failure in investment strategies, risk management, and forecasting. This is where Pandas, with its efficient and versatile data manipulation capabilities, becomes indispensable. Its contributions to financial data analysis are multifaceted, enabling professionals to handle complex datasets with precision and speed.

Handling Large Volumes of Data

Financial markets generate an enormous amount of data daily, from stock prices and trading volumes to economic indicators and corporate financial statements. Pandas excels in handling such large datasets, offering high-performance data structures and tools that facilitate quick and efficient data processing.

Consider a hedge fund analyst working in Vancouver who needs to analyze historical stock prices and trading volumes for multiple securities over decades. Using Pandas, the analyst can effortlessly import, clean, and manipulate this data, extracting valuable insights that inform investment decisions. The ability to manage large datasets efficiently is a game-changer, allowing financial professionals to keep pace with the fast-moving markets.

Data Cleaning and Preprocessing

One of the significant challenges in financial data analysis is dealing with incomplete or messy data. Missing values, inconsistent formats, and outliers can skew analysis and lead to erroneous conclusions. Pandas provides robust tools for data cleaning and preprocessing, enabling analysts to prepare datasets for accurate analysis.

For example, an investment banker in New York might be tasked with preparing financial statements from different companies for a merger analysis. These statements often come in various formats and contain missing values. Using Pandas, the banker can standardize these formats, fill or drop missing values, and ensure the dataset is clean and ready for analysis. This preprocessing step is crucial, as it ensures the integrity of the subsequent analysis and modeling.

Time Series Analysis

Financial data is inherently time-series data, where observations are collected at successive points in time. Analyzing this data requires specialized tools for handling and manipulating time indices. Pandas offers a suite of functionalities tailored for time series analysis, including date parsing, time-based indexing, resampling, and rolling window calculations.

Imagine a wealth manager in London tracking the performance of client portfolios. With Pandas, the manager can effortlessly parse dates, index data by time, and perform operations such as calculating moving averages or resampling data to different frequencies. This time series analysis capability is vital for uncovering trends, seasonality, and cyclic patterns in financial data, enabling more informed investment decisions.

Integration with Other Libraries

Pandas seamlessly integrates with other Python libraries, enhancing its utility in financial data analysis. For instance, it works hand-in-glove with NumPy for numerical computations, Matplotlib and Seaborn for data visualization, and Scikit-Learn for machine learning models. This interoperability allows analysts to build comprehensive workflows that cover the entire data analysis pipeline.

Consider a data scientist in a fintech startup developing predictive models for stock prices. By integrating Pandas with Scikit-Learn, the scientist can preprocess the data, train machine learning models, and evaluate their performance— all within a cohesive and efficient workflow. This seamless integration accelerates the analysis process and enables the development of sophisticated financial models.

Case Study: Analyzing Cryptocurrency Prices

To illustrate the importance of Pandas in financial data analysis, let's walk through a practical example involving cryptocurrency price analysis. Cryptocurrencies are known for their volatility, making them an exciting yet challenging asset class to analyze.

We'll start by importing historical price data for Bitcoin and Ethereum, calculating rolling averages, and visualizing the trends.

```python
```

```python
import pandas as pd
import matplotlib.pyplot as plt

# Read historical price data for Bitcoin and Ethereum
btc_data            =           pd.read_csv('bitcoin_prices.csv',
parse_dates=['Date'], index_col='Date')
eth_data            =           pd.read_csv('ethereum_prices.csv',
parse_dates=['Date'], index_col='Date')

# Calculate rolling averages
btc_data['30_day_MA']                                                =
btc_data['Close'].rolling(window=30).mean()
eth_data['30_day_MA']                                                =
eth_data['Close'].rolling(window=30).mean()

# Plot the prices and rolling averages
plt.figure(figsize=(14, 7))
plt.plot(btc_data['Close'],    label='Bitcoin    Close    Price',
color='blue')
plt.plot(btc_data['30_day_MA'], label='Bitcoin  30  Day  MA',
color='blue', linestyle='--')
plt.plot(eth_data['Close'],    label='Ethereum    Close    Price',
color='orange')
plt.plot(eth_data['30_day_MA'], label='Ethereum 30 Day MA',
color='orange', linestyle='--')
plt.title('Cryptocurrency Prices and Rolling Averages')
plt.xlabel('Date')
plt.ylabel('Price (USD)')
plt.legend()
plt.show()
```

` ` `

In this example, we first import the historical price data for Bitcoin and Ethereum into Pandas DataFrames. We then calculate the 30-day moving averages for the closing prices and plot the results. This analysis provides a clear visual representation of the price trends and moving averages, helping analysts identify patterns and make informed trading decisions.

Enhancing Decision-Making

Ultimately, the importance of Pandas in financial data analysis lies in its ability to enhance decision-making. By providing powerful tools for data manipulation, cleaning, time series analysis, and integration with other libraries, Pandas empowers financial professionals to extract meaningful insights from complex datasets. This leads to more accurate forecasts, better risk management, and more strategic investment decisions.

A portfolio manager in Toronto, for example, can leverage Pandas to analyze historical returns, optimize asset allocation, and backtest trading strategies. The insights gained from these analyses directly impact the manager's ability to achieve superior returns for clients, demonstrating the tangible value of Pandas in the financial industry.

Pandas is an essential tool for financial data analysis, offering unmatched capabilities for handling, manipulating, and analyzing financial datasets. Its contributions to data cleaning, time series analysis, and integration with other libraries make it a cornerstone of modern financial analysis workflows. As we continue through this book, you will learn how to harness the full power of Pandas to elevate your financial data analysis skills and drive better decision-making in your professional endeavors.

3. Installation and Setup of Pandas

In the competitive world of finance, every second counts. This makes the efficiency of your tools paramount. Therefore, setting up Pandas correctly from the outset will save you time and headaches in the long run. Let's walk through the process of installing and configuring Pandas, ensuring you're ready to dive into advanced financial data analysis without a hitch.

Installing Pandas

Pandas is a powerful, open-source data analysis and manipulation library for Python. To begin with Pandas, you need to have Python installed on your system. Python 3.6 or later is recommended for compatibility with the latest Pandas versions.

Step 1: Installing Python

If you don't already have Python installed, download it from the official website [python.org](https://www.python.org/downloads/). Follow the instructions for your specific operating system (Windows, macOS, or Linux). During installation, ensure you check the option to add Python to your system PATH, which makes it accessible from the command line.

Step 2: Installing Pandas via pip

The most straightforward way to install Pandas is using pip, Python's package installer. Open your command line interface (CLI) or terminal and type the following command:

```sh
pip install pandas
```

This command downloads and installs Pandas along with its dependencies, including NumPy, which is essential for numerical operations.

```sh
pip install pandas
```

For those using Anaconda, a distribution that simplifies package management and deployment, you can install Pandas via the conda package manager:

```sh
conda install pandas
```

Anaconda is particularly popular in data science and finance due to its extensive suite of pre-installed packages and user-friendly interface.

Verifying the Installation

After installation, it's good practice to verify that Pandas has been installed correctly. To do this, open a Python interpreter or Jupyter Notebook and execute the following code:

```python
import pandas as pd
print(pd.__version__)
```

If Pandas is installed correctly, this will print the version number, confirming that it is ready for use.

Setting Up Your Development Environment

A well-configured development environment can greatly enhance your productivity. Here are some tools and best practices to optimize your workflow for financial data analysis with Pandas.

Integrated Development Environment (IDE)

Choosing the right IDE can streamline your coding process. Some popular options include:

- PyCharm: Known for its powerful coding assistance and debugging features, PyCharm is a favorite among professionals.
- VSCode: Lightweight and highly customizable, Visual Studio Code offers numerous extensions for Python development.

- Jupyter Notebook: Ideal for interactive development and data analysis, Jupyter Notebook allows you to combine code, visualizations, and narrative text in a single document.

Each of these IDEs supports Pandas and offers unique features that can help you manage your projects more effectively.

Creating a Virtual Environment

Using a virtual environment isolates your project's dependencies, preventing conflicts between different projects and ensuring reproducibility. To create a virtual environment, navigate to your project directory in the CLI and run:

```sh
python -m venv myenv
```

Activate the virtual environment:

- On Windows:

```sh
myenv\Scripts\activate
```

- On macOS and Linux:

```sh
source myenv/bin/activate
```

Once activated, you can install Pandas and other necessary packages within this isolated environment.

Jupyter Notebook Setup

For interactive data analysis, Jupyter Notebook is indispensable. Installing Jupyter within your virtual environment ensures compatibility with your Pandas installation:

```sh
pip install jupyter
```

Launch Jupyter Notebook by typing:

```sh
jupyter notebook
```

This command opens Jupyter in your default web browser, where you can create and manage notebooks. Here's an example of initializing a Jupyter Notebook for financial data analysis:

```python
import pandas as pd

# Sample code to create a DataFrame
data = {'Date': ['2021-01-01', '2021-01-02', '2021-01-03'],
```

```
        'Close': [35000, 36000, 35500]}
df = pd.DataFrame(data)

# Display the DataFrame
df
```

This interactive environment allows you to test snippets of code and visualize data instantly, making it ideal for exploratory analysis.

Configuring Pandas for Performance

To ensure Pandas runs optimally, consider these configurations and best practices:

Setting Display Options

By default, Pandas limits the number of rows and columns displayed when printing a DataFrame. You can customize these settings to fit your needs:

```python
pd.set_option('display.max_rows', 100)
pd.set_option('display.max_columns', 50)
```

Adjusting these options allows you to view more data at a glance, which can be particularly useful when working with large financial datasets.

Improving Performance with Chunking

When dealing with extremely large datasets, reading data in chunks can prevent memory overload and improve performance. For instance, if you have a massive CSV file, you can read it in chunks:

```python
chunk_size = 100000
chunks = pd.read_csv('large_data.csv', chunksize=chunk_size)

for chunk in chunks:
    # Process each chunk
    process(chunk)
```

This method ensures that your system handles large datasets efficiently without running out of memory.

Utilizing Data Types

Specifying data types when reading data can significantly reduce memory usage:

```python
dtypes = {'column1': 'float32', 'column2': 'int32'}
data = pd.read_csv('data.csv', dtype=dtypes)
```

This approach is particularly beneficial when dealing with extensive financial datasets, as it optimizes memory consumption and speeds up processing.

With Pandas installed and your development environment finely tuned, you're now equipped to tackle advanced financial data analysis. This foundational setup is critical for ensuring that your tools run smoothly and efficiently, allowing you to focus on extracting valuable insights from your data without technical distractions. As we proceed to more complex topics, this solid groundwork will support your journey into the advanced functionalities of the Pandas library.

4. Basic Pandas Data Structures: Series and DataFrame

In the world of financial data analysis, a robust understanding of Pandas' fundamental data structures—Series and DataFrame—is essential. These two structures form the backbone of Pandas and provide a versatile framework for data manipulation and analysis, enabling you to handle vast amounts of financial information efficiently. Let's delve into the mechanics and applications of these foundational constructs.

Series: The One-Dimensional Data Structure

At its core, a Series is a one-dimensional array-like object that can hold various data types, including integers, floats, strings, and even complex numbers. Each element in a Series is associated with an index label, which allows for easy access and manipulation. Think of a Series as a column in a spreadsheet or a single dimension in a numpy array.

Creating a Series

Creating a Series is straightforward. You can initialize it with a list, a dictionary, or even a scalar value. Here's how you can create a Series from a list of stock prices:

```python
import pandas as pd

stock_prices = [150.0, 148.5, 152.3]
price_series = pd.Series(stock_prices, index=['AAPL', 'GOOG', 'AMZN'])
print(price_series)
```

This results in a Series with custom index labels:

```
AAPL   150.0
GOOG   148.5
AMZN   152.3
dtype: float64
```

The index labels (AAPL, GOOG, AMZN) allow for intuitive indexing and slicing, making data retrieval and manipulation efficient.

Accessing Data in a Series

You can access elements in a Series using the index labels or position. Here's an example of both methods:

```python
# Accessing by label
print(price_series['AAPL'])

# Accessing by position
print(price_series[0])
```

Both commands yield the same result—`150.0`, demonstrating the flexibility in accessing Series data.

Operations on Series

Series support a wide range of arithmetic operations, which are both intuitive and efficient. For instance, you can perform element-wise operations:

```python
# Increase each stock price by 1%
adjusted_prices = price_series * 1.01
print(adjusted_prices)
```

The result is:

```
AAPL   151.5
GOOG   149.985
AMZN   153.823
dtype: float64
```

These operations make it easy to perform calculations on financial data, such as adjusting prices, calculating returns, or applying custom transformations.

DataFrame: The Two-Dimensional Data Structure

While a Series is analogous to a column, a DataFrame is akin to a table in a database or a spreadsheet. It comprises multiple Series objects, each representing a column, and can hold diverse data types across columns.

Creating a DataFrame

You can create a DataFrame from various inputs, including dictionaries, lists, and other DataFrames. Here's an example of creating a DataFrame from a dictionary:

```python
data = {
    'Date': ['2021-01-01', '2021-01-02', '2021-01-03'],
    'AAPL': [150.0, 148.5, 152.3],
    'GOOG': [1725.0, 1710.3, 1730.0],
```

```
    'AMZN': [3180.0, 3155.5, 3200.8]
}

stock_df = pd.DataFrame(data)
print(stock_df)
```

This will output:

```
       Date  AAPL    GOOG    AMZN
0 2021-01-01 150.0  1725.0  3180.0
1 2021-01-02 148.5  1710.3  3155.5
2 2021-01-03 152.3  1730.0  3200.8
```

Accessing Data in a DataFrame

Accessing data in a DataFrame is versatile. You can retrieve columns, rows, or even specific elements using labels or positions:

```python
# Access a column
print(stock_df['AAPL'])

# Access a row by index
print(stock_df.loc[0])
```

```python
# Access a specific element
print(stock_df.at[0, 'AAPL'])
```

Manipulating DataFrame

DataFrames support a multitude of operations, enabling comprehensive data manipulation. Here's how you can add a new column, modify existing data, and drop columns:

```python
# Adding a new column for percentage change
stock_df['AAPL_Pct_Change'] = stock_df['AAPL'].pct_change()
print(stock_df)

# Modifying existing data
stock_df.at[1, 'AAPL'] = 149.0
print(stock_df)

# Dropping a column
stock_df = stock_df.drop(columns=['AAPL_Pct_Change'])
print(stock_df)
```

These operations showcase the ease with which you can augment and refine your datasets, crucial for financial analysis and reporting.

Real-world Application: Analyzing Financial Data

To highlight the practical use of Series and DataFrame, let's walk through a real-world example. Suppose you want to analyze historical stock prices for a portfolio of companies. You can start by importing data from a CSV file:

```python
# Reading stock data from a CSV file
stock_data = pd.read_csv('historical_stock_prices.csv', parse_dates=['Date'])

# Display the first few rows
print(stock_data.head())
```

This initial step is vital for loading your dataset into a structured format. Next, you can perform various analyses, such as calculating daily returns:

```python
# Calculating daily returns
stock_data['AAPL_Returns'] = stock_data['AAPL'].pct_change()
stock_data['GOOG_Returns'] = stock_data['GOOG'].pct_change()
stock_data['AMZN_Returns'] = stock_data['AMZN'].pct_change()

# Display the modified DataFrame
print(stock_data.head())
```

Here, the `pct_change()` function computes the percentage change between the current and previous row, enabling you to analyze stock performance over time.

Advanced Techniques: Hierarchical Indexing

Pandas also supports hierarchical indexing, allowing you to work with datasets that have multi-level indexing. This is particularly useful for multi-dimensional financial data, such as stock prices over different time periods and companies:

```python
# Creating a MultiIndex DataFrame
arrays = [
    ['AAPL', 'AAPL', 'GOOG', 'GOOG', 'AMZN', 'AMZN'],
    ['Open', 'Close', 'Open', 'Close', 'Open', 'Close']
]
index = pd.MultiIndex.from_arrays(arrays, names=('Stock', 'Type'))
data = [
    [150.0, 148.0, 1725.0, 1710.0, 3180.0, 3155.0],
    [148.5, 150.0, 1710.3, 1725.3, 3155.5, 3170.8]
]
multi_df = pd.DataFrame(data, columns=index)

# Display the MultiIndex DataFrame
print(multi_df)
```

This results in a DataFrame with hierarchical indexing, enabling sophisticated data queries and manipulations:

```
` ` `
Stock AAPL    GOOG    AMZN
Type  Open Close Open Close Open Close
0    150.0 148.0 1725.0 1710.0 3180.0 3155.0
1    148.5 150.0 1710.3 1725.3 3155.5 3170.8
` ` `
```

Hierarchical indexing simplifies the management of complex financial datasets, facilitating advanced analytical tasks and visualizations.

5. Reading Financial Data Using Pandas

Reading Data from CSV Files

CSV (Comma-Separated Values) files are one of the most common formats for storing and exchanging financial data. Pandas provides the `read_csv()` function to load CSV files into DataFrames efficiently.

Example: Reading Stock Prices from a CSV File

Imagine you have a CSV file named `stock_prices.csv` containing historical stock prices. Here's how you can read this file into a Pandas DataFrame:

```python
import pandas as pd

# Reading the CSV file
file_path = 'stock_prices.csv'
stock_data = pd.read_csv(file_path)

# Displaying the first few rows of the DataFrame
print(stock_data.head())
```

This simple code snippet reads the CSV file and outputs the first few rows of the DataFrame, giving you a quick glimpse of your dataset. The `pd.read_csv()` function is highly versatile, with parameters to handle various data nuances like date parsing, missing values, and custom delimiters.

Handling Dates During Import

Financial data often includes date columns that are crucial for time series analysis. Pandas can automatically parse these dates during the import process using the `parse_dates` parameter.

```python
# Reading the CSV file with date parsing
stock_data = pd.read_csv(file_path, parse_dates=['Date'])

# Displaying the first few rows of the DataFrame
print(stock_data.head())
```

```
` ` `
```

In this example, the `Date` column is parsed as a datetime object, enabling you to leverage Pandas' powerful time series functionalities right from the outset.

Reading Data from Excel Files

Excel is widely used in the financial industry for data storage and analysis. Pandas offers the `read_excel()` function to read data from Excel spreadsheets.

Example: Reading Financial Statements from an Excel File

Suppose you have an Excel file named `financial_statements.xlsx` with multiple sheets for different financial statements. Here's how you can read data from a specific sheet:

```python
# Reading data from the 'Income Statement' sheet
income_statement = pd.read_excel('financial_statements.xlsx', sheet_name='Income Statement')

# Displaying the first few rows of the DataFrame
print(income_statement.head())
```

The `sheet_name` parameter allows you to specify the sheet you want to read. If you need to read multiple sheets, you can pass a list of sheet names or use `sheet_name=None` to read all sheets into a dictionary of DataFrames.

Importing Data from SQL Databases

For larger datasets and more complex queries, SQL databases are often the preferred choice. Pandas integrates seamlessly with SQL databases through the `read_sql()` function.

Example: Importing Stock Data from a SQL Database

Consider a scenario where your stock data is stored in a SQL database. Here's how you can read this data into a Pandas DataFrame:

```python
import sqlite3

# Establishing a connection to the database
conn = sqlite3.connect('financial_data.db')

# Reading data from the 'stocks' table
query = 'SELECT * FROM stocks'
stocks_df = pd.read_sql(query, conn)

# Displaying the first few rows of the DataFrame
print(stocks_df.head())
```

This approach enables you to execute SQL queries directly and import the results into Pandas, offering a powerful way to filter and aggregate data before analysis.

Fetching Real-Time Data from APIs

In today's fast-paced financial markets, accessing real-time data is crucial. Many financial data providers offer APIs that you can use to fetch up-to-the-minute market data. Libraries like `requests` and `yfinance` can be used alongside Pandas to achieve this.

Example: Fetching Real-Time Stock Prices Using the yfinance Library

The `yfinance` library provides a straightforward interface to fetch real-time stock prices from Yahoo Finance. Here's how you can use it to download stock data:

```python
import yfinance as yf

# Fetching stock data for Apple Inc. (AAPL)
aapl_data = yf.download('AAPL', start='2022-01-01', end='2022-12-31')

# Displaying the first few rows of the DataFrame
print(aapl_data.head())
```

This example downloads historical stock data for Apple Inc. for the year 2022 and loads it into a Pandas DataFrame. You can easily adjust the ticker symbol and date range to fetch data for different stocks and time periods.

Reading Data from JSON Files

JSON (JavaScript Object Notation) files are also widely used to store financial data, especially when interacting with web APIs. Pandas provides the `read_json()` function to read JSON files or JSON strings into DataFrames.

Example: Reading Financial Data from a JSON File

Suppose you have a JSON file named `financial_data.json` containing financial metrics. Here's how you can read this file into a DataFrame:

```python
# Reading the JSON file
financial_data = pd.read_json('financial_data.json')

# Displaying the first few rows of the DataFrame
print(financial_data.head())
```

The `read_json()` function handles various JSON formats, making it easy to integrate JSON-based data sources into your analysis workflow.

Practical Application: Combining Data from Multiple Sources

In real-world financial analysis, you often need to combine data from multiple sources to get a comprehensive view. Pandas excels at this by providing functions to merge, join, and concatenate DataFrames.

Example: Merging CSV and API Data

Let's say you have historical stock prices in a CSV file and want to enrich it with real-time data fetched from an API. Here's how you can achieve this:

```python
# Reading historical stock prices from a CSV file
historical_data = pd.read_csv('historical_stock_prices.csv', parse_dates=['Date'])

# Fetching real-time stock prices using yfinance
real_time_data = yf.download('AAPL', start='2023-01-01', end='2023-01-31')

# Merging the two DataFrames on the 'Date' column
combined_data = pd.merge(historical_data, real_time_data, on='Date', how='outer')

# Displaying the first few rows of the combined DataFrame
print(combined_data.head())
```

In this example, the `pd.merge()` function combines historical and real-time stock data on the `Date` column, giving you a unified dataset for comprehensive analysis.

Reading and integrating financial data from various sources is a fundamental skill for any financial analyst. Pandas provides a robust set of tools to handle CSV files, Excel spreadsheets,

SQL databases, real-time APIs, and JSON files, making data ingestion seamless and efficient. With these capabilities, you'll be well-equipped to tackle diverse datasets, ensuring that your analysis is based on comprehensive and up-to-date information. As you continue to build on this foundation, you'll find that Pandas' data ingestion functionalities are indispensable for sophisticated financial data analysis.

6. Data Cleaning and Preprocessing in Pandas

Identifying and Handling Missing Data

Missing data is a common issue in financial datasets. Pandas offers several methods to identify and handle these gaps, ensuring the integrity of your analysis.

Example: Detecting Missing Values

Let's start by identifying missing values in a dataset:

```python
import pandas as pd

# Creating a sample DataFrame with missing values
data = {'Date': ['2023-01-01', '2023-01-02', '2023-01-03', '2023-01-04'],
        'Stock Price': [150, None, 152, 153]}
df = pd.DataFrame(data)
```

```
# Checking for missing values
print(df.isnull())
print(df.isnull().sum())
```

The `isnull()` function returns a DataFrame of the same shape as `df`, indicating the presence of missing values, while `isnull().sum()` provides a count of missing values in each column.

Handling Missing Values

There are multiple strategies to handle missing values, including removal, imputation, or forward/backward filling.

Method 1: Removing Missing Values

```python
# Dropping rows with missing values
df_dropped = df.dropna()

# Displaying the cleaned DataFrame
print(df_dropped)
```

The `dropna()` function removes any rows with missing values, resulting in a cleaner dataset.

Method 2: Imputation

Imputation involves replacing missing values with a specific value, such as the mean, median, or a forward/backward fill.

```python
# Filling missing values with the mean
df_filled_mean = df.fillna(df['Stock Price'].mean())

# Forward filling missing values
df_ffill = df.fillna(method='ffill')

# Backward filling missing values
df_bfill = df.fillna(method='bfill')

print(df_filled_mean)
print(df_ffill)
print(df_bfill)
```

In this example, we demonstrate three imputation methods: filling with the mean, forward filling (propagating the last valid observation forward), and backward filling (propagating the next valid observation backward).

Removing Duplicates

Duplicate records can distort your analysis. Pandas provides the `drop_duplicates()` function to identify and remove these redundancies.

```python
```

```python
# Creating a sample DataFrame with duplicate rows
data = {'Date': ['2023-01-01', '2023-01-02', '2023-01-02',
'2023-01-03'],
        'Stock Price': [150, 151, 151, 152]}
df = pd.DataFrame(data)

# Removing duplicate rows
df_no_duplicates = df.drop_duplicates()

# Displaying the cleaned DataFrame
print(df_no_duplicates)
```

The `drop_duplicates()` function removes duplicate rows, ensuring that each record in your dataset is unique.

Correcting Data Types

Financial datasets often contain columns with incorrect data types. Pandas allows you to convert these columns to appropriate types, facilitating accurate computations and analysis.

```python
# Creating a sample DataFrame with incorrect data types
data = {'Date': ['2023-01-01', '2023-01-02', '2023-01-03'],
        'Stock Price': ['150', '151', '152']}
df = pd.DataFrame(data)

# Converting 'Date' column to datetime
```

```
df['Date'] = pd.to_datetime(df['Date'])

# Converting 'Stock Price' column to numeric
df['Stock Price'] = pd.to_numeric(df['Stock Price'])

# Displaying the cleaned DataFrame
print(df.dtypes)
```

In this example, we convert the `Date` column to datetime format and the `Stock Price` column to a numeric type, ensuring that the data is in a suitable format for further analysis.

Handling Outliers

Outliers can significantly impact financial analysis. Pandas, combined with visualization libraries like Matplotlib, helps identify and address these anomalies.

Detecting Outliers Using Visualization

```python
import matplotlib.pyplot as plt

# Creating a sample DataFrame with outliers
data = {'Date': pd.date_range(start='2023-01-01', periods=10),
        'Stock Price': [150, 152, 151, 148, 149, 300, 147, 148, 149, 150]}
df = pd.DataFrame(data)
```

```python
# Plotting the data
plt.plot(df['Date'], df['Stock Price'])
plt.xlabel('Date')
plt.ylabel('Stock Price')
plt.title('Stock Prices Over Time')
plt.show()
```

This line plot helps visualize the presence of an outlier (300) in the `Stock Price` column.

Handling Outliers

Outliers can be handled by removing them or transforming them.

```python
# Removing outliers
q1 = df['Stock Price'].quantile(0.25)
q3 = df['Stock Price'].quantile(0.75)
iqr = q3 - q1
lower_bound = q1 - 1.5 * iqr
upper_bound = q3 + 1.5 * iqr

df_cleaned = df[(df['Stock Price'] >= lower_bound) & (df['Stock Price'] <= upper_bound)]

# Displaying the cleaned DataFrame
```

```
print(df_cleaned)
```
```
```

Using the interquartile range (IQR) method, we identify and remove outliers, ensuring the dataset accurately represents the underlying patterns without distortion.

Standardizing and Normalizing Data

Standardizing or normalizing data is often necessary to ensure comparability, especially when dealing with multiple datasets or models that assume data in a particular format.

Standardization

Standardization rescales the data to have a mean of 0 and a standard deviation of 1.

```python
from sklearn.preprocessing import StandardScaler

# Creating a sample DataFrame
data = {'Stock Price': [150, 152, 151, 148, 149, 147, 148, 149, 150]}
df = pd.DataFrame(data)

# Standardizing the data
scaler = StandardScaler()
df['Standardized'] = scaler.fit_transform(df[['Stock Price']])

# Displaying the standardized DataFrame
```

```
print(df)
```
` ` `

In this example, the `StandardScaler` from `sklearn.preprocessing` standardizes the `Stock Price` column.

Normalization

Normalization rescales the data to a range of [0, 1].

` ` `python
```python
from sklearn.preprocessing import MinMaxScaler

# Normalizing the data
scaler = MinMaxScaler()
df['Normalized'] = scaler.fit_transform(df[['Stock Price']])

# Displaying the normalized DataFrame
print(df)
```
` ` `

Similarly, the `MinMaxScaler` normalizes the `Stock Price` column to a 0-1 range, useful for models sensitive to data scales.

Practical Application: Cleaning a Real-World Financial Dataset

Let's put these techniques into practice by cleaning a real-world financial dataset.

Example: Cleaning a Dataset of Historical Stock Prices

Consider a CSV file named `historical_stock_prices.csv` containing historical stock price data. We will clean this dataset by handling missing values, removing duplicates, correcting data types, and standardizing the data.

```python
# Reading the CSV file
file_path = 'historical_stock_prices.csv'
df = pd.read_csv(file_path, parse_dates=['Date'])

# Handling missing values by forward filling
df = df.fillna(method='ffill')

# Removing duplicate rows
df = df.drop_duplicates()

# Correcting data types
df['Stock Price'] = pd.to_numeric(df['Stock Price'])

# Standardizing the stock prices
scaler = StandardScaler()
df['Standardized Stock Price'] = scaler.fit_transform(df[['Stock Price']])

# Displaying the cleaned DataFrame
print(df.head())
```

Combining the techniques discussed, we transform the raw dataset into a clean and standardized format, ready for sophisticated analysis.

Data cleaning and preprocessing are critical steps in financial data analysis, ensuring the accuracy and reliability of your insights. Pandas offers a comprehensive toolkit to handle missing values, remove duplicates, correct data types, address outliers, and standardize data. Mastering these techniques equips you to tackle the complexities of financial datasets, laying a solid foundation for advanced analysis and modeling. As you progress through this book, these skills will prove invaluable in extracting meaningful insights from your financial data.

7. Handling Missing Data in Financial Datasets

In the world of finance, dealing with missing data is an unavoidable and challenging task. Financial datasets, whether they come from stock markets, historical economic indicators, or corporate financial statements, often contain gaps. These missing values can arise due to various reasons, such as data entry errors, system failures, or simply unrecorded events. To ensure the integrity and reliability of your analyses, it's crucial to handle missing data appropriately. Pandas provides a comprehensive suite of tools to detect, analyze, and manage missing data efficiently.

Identifying Missing Data

The first step in handling missing data is to identify where the gaps are. Pandas offers several methods to detect missing values, which are typically represented as `NaN` (Not a Number).

Example: Detecting Missing Values

Consider a dataset of daily stock prices:

```python
import pandas as pd

# Creating a sample DataFrame with missing values
data = {'Date': ['2023-01-01', '2023-01-02', '2023-01-03', '2023-01-04'],
        'Stock Price': [150, None, 152, 153]}
df = pd.DataFrame(data)

# Checking for missing values
print(df.isnull())
print(df.isnull().sum())
```

The `isnull()` function returns a DataFrame of the same shape as `df`, with `True` indicating the presence of a missing value, while `isnull().sum()` provides a count of missing values in each column. Identifying the extent and pattern of missing data is essential for deciding how to handle it.

Handling Missing Values

Once you have identified the missing values, there are several strategies to address them. These include removing, imputing, or filling the missing values. The choice of method depends on the nature of your data and the analysis you intend to perform.

Method 1: Removing Missing Values

Removing missing values is a straightforward approach, but it can lead to data loss, especially if a significant portion of your dataset is incomplete.

```python
# Dropping rows with missing values
df_dropped = df.dropna()

# Displaying the cleaned DataFrame
print(df_dropped)
```

The `dropna()` function removes any rows containing missing values, resulting in a cleaner DataFrame. However, use this method with caution as it may lead to substantial data loss.

Method 2: Imputation

Imputation involves replacing missing values with other values, such as the mean, median, or mode of the column. This method retains all data points and can be useful for maintaining the overall dataset structure.

Example: Filling Missing Values with Mean

```python
# Filling missing values with the column mean
df_filled_mean = df.copy()
df_filled_mean['Stock Price'] = df['Stock Price'].fillna(df['Stock Price'].mean())

print(df_filled_mean)
```

In this example, the missing values in the `Stock Price` column are replaced with the mean of the column, preserving the overall dataset.

Forward and Backward Filling

Forward and backward filling propagate the last valid observation or the next valid observation, respectively, to fill missing values.

```python
# Forward filling missing values
df_ffill = df.fillna(method='ffill')

# Backward filling missing values
df_bfill = df.fillna(method='bfill')

print(df_ffill)
```

```
print(df_bfill)
` ` `
```

Forward filling fills missing values with the last non-missing value, while backward filling uses the next non-missing value. These methods are useful when the missing data points are isolated.

Analyzing Patterns of Missing Data

Understanding the pattern of missing data is crucial for choosing the appropriate handling method. Visualizations can help identify patterns and correlations in missing data.

Example: Visualizing Missing Data

```python
import seaborn as sns
import matplotlib.pyplot as plt

# Creating a larger sample DataFrame with missing values
data = {'Date': pd.date_range(start='2023-01-01', periods=10),
        'Stock Price': [150, None, 152, None, 153, 154, None, 155, 156, None]}
df = pd.DataFrame(data)

# Visualizing missing values
sns.heatmap(df.isnull(), cbar=False, cmap='viridis')
plt.title('Missing Data Heatmap')
plt.show()
```

` ` `

This heatmap visually represents missing values in the dataset, allowing you to see any patterns or clusters of missing data.

Advanced Imputation Techniques

For more sophisticated handling of missing data, advanced imputation techniques can be employed, such as interpolation or model-based imputation. These methods can provide more accurate imputations based on the underlying data structure.

Example: Interpolation

Interpolation estimates missing values by using the surrounding data points. Pandas offers several interpolation methods.

```python
# Linear interpolation
df_interpolated = df.copy()
df_interpolated['Stock Price']       =       df['Stock Price'].interpolate(method='linear')

print(df_interpolated)
```

Linear interpolation fills missing values by estimating them based on the previous and next values. This method is particularly useful for time series data.

Model-Based Imputation

Machine learning models can also be used for imputing missing values by predicting them based on other features in the dataset.

```python
from sklearn.impute import KNNImputer

# Creating a sample DataFrame with additional feature
data = {'Date': pd.date_range(start='2023-01-01', periods=10),
        'Stock Price': [150, None, 152, None, 153, 154, None, 155, 156, None],
        'Volume': [1000, 1100, 1050, 1200, 1300, 1250, 1400, 1350, 1450, 1500]}
df = pd.DataFrame(data)

# Using KNNImputer for imputation
imputer = KNNImputer(n_neighbors=2)
df[['Stock Price', 'Volume']] = imputer.fit_transform(df[['Stock Price', 'Volume']])

print(df)
```

The `KNNImputer` from `sklearn.impute` uses the k-nearest neighbors algorithm to fill missing values, leveraging the correlation between `Stock Price` and `Volume`.

Practical Application: Handling Missing Data in Market Indices

Consider a dataset containing historical market index data with missing values. We will apply the techniques discussed to handle the missing data.

Example: Cleaning a Market Index Dataset

```python
# Reading the market index dataset
file_path = 'market_indices.csv'
df = pd.read_csv(file_path, parse_dates=['Date'])

# Visualizing missing values
sns.heatmap(df.isnull(), cbar=False, cmap='viridis')
plt.title('Missing Data Heatmap')
plt.show()

# Filling missing values with forward fill
df = df.fillna(method='ffill')

# Dropping any remaining rows with missing values
df = df.dropna()

# Displaying the cleaned DataFrame
print(df.head())
```

Combining visualization and imputation techniques, we can clean the dataset effectively, ensuring that it is ready for further analysis.

Handling missing data is a crucial step in preparing financial datasets for analysis. Pandas provides a versatile set of tools to detect, analyze, and manage missing values. Whether through simple methods like removal and basic imputation or advanced techniques like interpolation and machine learning-based imputation, mastering these skills ensures that your dataset is reliable and your analysis is robust. As you continue to work with financial data, these techniques will become indispensable in your toolkit, enabling you to handle incomplete datasets with confidence and precision.

8. Overview of Financial Datasets (Stocks, Bonds, Crypto, etc.)

Stocks: Equity Market Data

Stock data represents ownership in publicly traded companies, providing information about share prices, trading volumes, dividends, and corporate actions. Analysts rely heavily on stock market data for various purposes, including price trend analysis, risk assessment, and portfolio management.

Structure of Stock Data

A typical stock dataset includes:

- Date: The trading date.
- Open: The price at which the stock opened for trading.
- High: The highest price during the trading session.
- Low: The lowest price during the trading session.

- Close: The price at which the stock closed.

- Volume: The number of shares traded during the session.

- Adjusted Close: The closing price adjusted for corporate actions like splits and dividends.

Example: Reading Stock Data with Pandas

```python
import pandas as pd

# Reading stock data from a CSV file
file_path = 'stock_data.csv'
stock_df = pd.read_csv(file_path, parse_dates=['Date'])

# Displaying the first few rows of the dataset
print(stock_df.head())
```

In this example, stock data is read from a CSV file, and the `Date` column is parsed as datetime objects for easier manipulation.

Bonds: Fixed Income Securities

Bonds are debt instruments issued by governments, municipalities, and corporations to finance their operations and projects. Bond data includes details about the issuer, face value, coupon rate, maturity date, and yield.

Structure of Bond Data

A typical bond dataset comprises:

- Date: The trading date.
- Issuer: The entity that issued the bond.
- Coupon Rate: The interest rate paid by the bond.
- Maturity Date: The date when the bond's principal is repaid.
- Face Value: The bond's nominal value.
- Yield: The bond's effective return rate.

Example: Reading Bond Data with Pandas

```python
# Reading bond data from a CSV file
file_path = 'bond_data.csv'
bond_df = pd.read_csv(file_path, parse_dates=['Date', 'Maturity Date'])

# Displaying the first few rows of the dataset
print(bond_df.head())
```

In this example, bond data is read from a CSV file, with both the `Date` and `Maturity Date` columns parsed as datetime objects.

Cryptocurrencies: Digital Asset Data

Cryptocurrencies, such as Bitcoin and Ethereum, represent digital or virtual assets that use cryptographic technologies for secure transactions. Cryptocurrency data is characterized by high volatility and is often used for speculative trading, portfolio diversification, and technological innovation studies.

Structure of Cryptocurrency Data

A typical cryptocurrency dataset includes:

- Date: The trading date.
- Open: The opening price.
- High: The highest price during the trading session.
- Low: The lowest price during the trading session.
- Close: The closing price.
- Volume: The trading volume.
- Market Cap: The total market capitalization.

Example: Reading Cryptocurrency Data with Pandas

```python
# Reading cryptocurrency data from a JSON file
file_path = 'crypto_data.json'
crypto_df = pd.read_json(file_path)

# Displaying the first few rows of the dataset
print(crypto_df.head())
```

Cryptocurrency data can often be found in JSON format, which can be easily read and parsed using Pandas.

Commodities: Market Data for Goods

Commodities include physical goods such as gold, oil, and agricultural products. Commodity data is essential for understanding the supply and demand dynamics of these goods and is used for hedging, speculative trading, and economic analysis.

Structure of Commodity Data

A typical commodity dataset includes:

- Date: The trading date.
- Open: The opening price.
- High: The highest price during the trading session.
- Low: The lowest price during the trading session.
- Close: The closing price.
- Volume: The trading volume.

Example: Reading Commodity Data with Pandas

```python
# Reading commodity data from an Excel file
file_path = 'commodity_data.xlsx'
commodity_df = pd.read_excel(file_path, parse_dates=['Date'])

# Displaying the first few rows of the dataset
print(commodity_df.head())
```

Commodity data is often stored in Excel files and can be read using the `read_excel` method from Pandas.

Foreign Exchange (Forex): Currency Market Data

Forex data represents the exchange rates between different currencies and is fundamental for international trade, investment, and economic policy analysis. Forex datasets are highly dynamic and influenced by geopolitical events, economic indicators, and market sentiment.

Structure of Forex Data

A typical forex dataset includes:

- Date: The trading date.
- Currency Pair: The currencies being exchanged (e.g., EUR/USD).
- Open: The opening exchange rate.
- High: The highest exchange rate during the trading session.
- Low: The lowest exchange rate during the trading session.
- Close: The closing exchange rate.
- Volume: The trading volume.

Example: Reading Forex Data with Pandas

```python
# Reading forex data from a CSV file
file_path = 'forex_data.csv'
```

```
forex_df = pd.read_csv(file_path, parse_dates=['Date'])

# Displaying the first few rows of the dataset
print(forex_df.head())
```
` ` `

In this example, forex data is read from a CSV file, and the `Date` column is parsed as datetime objects.

Integrating Multiple Financial Datasets

In real-world financial analysis, integrating multiple datasets is common. For instance, combining stock and bond data can provide a comprehensive view of an investment portfolio's performance. Pandas offers robust functionalities for merging and joining datasets, enabling seamless integration.

Example: Merging Stock and Bond Data

` ` `python
```
# Merging stock and bond data on the Date column
merged_df = pd.merge(stock_df, bond_df, on='Date', suffixes=('_stock', '_bond'))

# Displaying the first few rows of the merged dataset
print(merged_df.head())
```
` ` `

In this example, stock and bond data are merged on the `Date` column, providing a unified view of both datasets.

Understanding the structure, sources, and typical use cases of various financial datasets is the cornerstone of effective financial analysis. Whether dealing with stocks, bonds, cryptocurrencies, commodities, or forex, each dataset presents unique opportunities and challenges. Mastering the ability to read, manipulate, and integrate these diverse datasets using Pandas equips you with the tools to perform comprehensive and insightful analyses, driving informed decision-making in the dynamic world of finance.

Pandas Integration with Other Python Libraries

NumPy: Enhancing Numerical Operations

NumPy (Numerical Python) forms the backbone of numerical computations in Python. Pandas is inherently built upon NumPy, utilizing its capabilities for efficient data storage and manipulation through its arrays. The tight coupling between Pandas and NumPy allows for seamless integration.

Consider the scenario where you need to perform element-wise mathematical operations on large financial datasets. NumPy excels in these tasks due to its fast, memory-efficient operations. By converting Pandas DataFrames to NumPy arrays, you can leverage NumPy's vast array of functions to process your data more effectively.

```python
import pandas as pd
import numpy as np

# Create a sample DataFrame
```

```
data = {'Stock_A': [100, 110, 105, 120],
        'Stock_B': [95, 100, 102, 110]}
df = pd.DataFrame(data)

# Convert DataFrame to NumPy array for element-wise
operations
arr = df.values
arr_normalized = arr / arr.mean(axis=0)

# Convert the result back to DataFrame
df_normalized       =       pd.DataFrame(arr_normalized,
columns=df.columns)
print(df_normalized)
` ` `
```

In this example, we normalized stock prices by dividing them by their mean values, showcasing how transforming between Pandas DataFrames and NumPy arrays can be employed for efficient numerical operations.

Matplotlib and Seaborn: Visualizing Financial Data

Visualization is an indispensable tool in financial data analysis, making trends and patterns discernible at a glance. While Pandas has basic plotting capabilities, integrating with Matplotlib and Seaborn opens up advanced visualization options.

Matplotlib is the de facto standard for creating static, interactive, and animated visualizations in Python. Seaborn, built on top of Matplotlib, provides a high-level interface for drawing attractive statistical graphics. The combination of these libraries can dramatically enhance the visual representation of your financial data.

```python
import matplotlib.pyplot as plt
import seaborn as sns

# Plotting using Matplotlib and Seaborn
plt.figure(figsize=(10, 6))
sns.lineplot(data=df)
plt.title('Stock Prices Over Time')
plt.xlabel('Days')
plt.ylabel('Price')
plt.legend(df.columns)
plt.show()
```

Here, we used Seaborn to plot line graphs of stock prices, allowing for clear, aesthetically pleasing visualizations that can be customized extensively using Matplotlib.

SciPy: Advanced Statistical Analysis

SciPy (Scientific Python) extends NumPy's capabilities by adding a collection of algorithms and functions for scientific and technical computing. For financial analysts, SciPy offers advanced statistical functions, optimization techniques, and signal processing tools that are vital for in-depth analysis.

For instance, performing a linear regression to understand the relationship between two financial variables can be easily achieved using SciPy.

```python
from scipy import stats

# Example data for regression
x = np.array([1, 2, 3, 4, 5])
y = np.array([2.2, 2.8, 3.6, 4.5, 5.1])

# Perform linear regression
slope, intercept, r_value, p_value, std_err = stats.linregress(x, y)

print(f"Slope: {slope}, Intercept: {intercept}, R-squared: {r_value2}")
```

This script demonstrates how to perform a linear regression analysis, providing valuable insights into trends and relationships within financial datasets.

Statsmodels: Detailed Statistical Modeling

Statsmodels is another powerful library for statistical modeling and hypothesis testing. It complements Pandas by providing classes and functions to estimate and analyze several types of statistical models. This is particularly useful for time series analysis, regression, and forecasting in finance.

Consider an ARIMA (AutoRegressive Integrated Moving Average) model for time series forecasting:

```python
import statsmodels.api as sm

# Sample time series data
ts_data = pd.Series([112, 118, 132, 129, 121, 135, 148, 148, 136, 119],
                    index=pd.date_range(start='2022-01-01', periods=10, freq='M'))

# Fit ARIMA model
model = sm.tsa.ARIMA(ts_data, order=(1, 1, 1))
results = model.fit()

print(results.summary())
```

Here, we fit an ARIMA model to a sample time series, showcasing the ease with which complex statistical models can be implemented using Statsmodels.

Scikit-learn: Machine Learning Models

Scikit-learn is the go-to library for machine learning in Python. Its integration with Pandas makes it straightforward to preprocess data, train models, and evaluate their performance. Whether you're predicting stock prices or classifying financial transactions, Scikit-learn offers a comprehensive suite of tools.

An example of using Scikit-learn for a simple classification task:

```python
from sklearn.model_selection import train_test_split
from sklearn.ensemble import RandomForestClassifier
from sklearn.metrics import accuracy_score

# Sample dataset
data = {'feature1': [1, 2, 3, 4, 5],
        'feature2': [5, 4, 3, 2, 1],
        'label': [0, 1, 0, 1, 0]}
df = pd.DataFrame(data)

# Preparing the data for training
X = df[['feature1', 'feature2']]
y = df['label']
X_train, X_test, y_train, y_test = train_test_split(X, y,
test_size=0.2, random_state=42)

# Training a Random Forest Classifier
clf         =           RandomForestClassifier(n_estimators=100,
random_state=42)
clf.fit(X_train, y_train)
y_pred = clf.predict(X_test)

# Evaluating the model
accuracy = accuracy_score(y_test, y_pred)
print(f"Model Accuracy: {accuracy}")
```

In this example, we trained a Random Forest classifier to

predict a binary label, demonstrating how seamlessly Scikit-learn integrates with Pandas for machine learning tasks.

SQLAlchemy: Database Integration

Financial data often resides in databases, and SQLAlchemy is the bridge that connects Pandas with SQL databases. By leveraging SQLAlchemy, you can seamlessly read from and write to SQL databases, integrating Pandas DataFrames directly with your existing database infrastructure.

```python
from sqlalchemy import create_engine

# Create an SQLite engine
engine = create_engine('sqlite:///financial_data.db')

# Reading data from SQL
df_sql = pd.read_sql('SELECT * FROM stock_prices', con=engine)

# Writing data to SQL
df.to_sql('normalized_stock_prices', con=engine, if_exists='replace', index=False)
```

Here, we connected to an SQLite database, read data into a Pandas DataFrame, and wrote data back to the database, illustrating the ease of database integration with Pandas.

Integrating Pandas with these powerful Python libraries, you create a comprehensive environment for financial data analysis, enhancing your ability to handle complex datasets, perform advanced analyses, and generate meaningful insights. Each integration offers unique strengths, allowing you to leverage the full spectrum of Python's capabilities in your financial analysis tasks.

Introduction to Jupyter Notebook for Financial Analysis

What is Jupyter Notebook?

Jupyter Notebook is an open-source web application that allows you to create and share documents containing live code, equations, visualizations, and narrative text. It supports multiple programming languages, including Python, which makes it an ideal tool for financial analysts who often rely on Python's data analysis libraries.

The core of Jupyter Notebook is its interactive nature, which enables analysts to write code, execute it, and see the results in real-time. This interaction not only accelerates the workflow but also facilitates the exploration and visualization of financial data.

Setting Up Jupyter Notebook

Before diving into the functionalities of Jupyter Notebook, it's essential to set it up on your system. The easiest way to install Jupyter Notebook is through the Anaconda distribution, which packages Jupyter along with other essential data science libraries.

1. Install Anaconda:

Download and install Anaconda from [Anaconda's official website](https://www.anaconda.com/products/distribution). Anaconda simplifies package management and deployment, making it easier to set up the necessary tools for financial analysis.

2. Launch Jupyter Notebook:

Once Anaconda is installed, you can launch Jupyter Notebook from the Anaconda Navigator or by running the following command in your terminal or command prompt:

```bash
jupyter notebook
```

Navigating the Jupyter Notebook Interface

After launching Jupyter Notebook, you will be greeted by the Notebook Dashboard, which displays the contents of your current directory. From here, you can create new notebooks, open existing ones, and manage your files.

1. Creating a New Notebook:

To create a new notebook, click on the "New" button and select "Python 3" (or your preferred programming language). This opens a new notebook with an empty cell where you can start writing and executing code.

2. The Notebook Layout:

A Jupyter Notebook is composed of cells, which can contain code, markdown text, or raw text. Each cell can be executed independently, and the output is displayed directly below the cell. This layout is particularly useful for iterative analysis and experimentation.

3. Running Cells:

To execute the code in a cell, press `Shift + Enter`. The output of the cell's computation will appear directly beneath it. This immediate feedback loop is a key feature of Jupyter Notebook and enhances the exploratory data analysis process.

Using Jupyter Notebook for Financial Data Analysis

Jupyter Notebook excels in performing data analysis tasks, especially when combined with libraries such as Pandas, Matplotlib, and Seaborn. Let's explore how Jupyter Notebook can be used to conduct a comprehensive financial analysis.

1. Loading Financial Data:

Begin by importing the necessary libraries and loading your financial dataset into a Pandas DataFrame. For example, let's load historical stock price data from a CSV file:

```python
import pandas as pd

# Load the dataset
df = pd.read_csv('historical_stock_prices.csv')
df.head()
```

2. Data Cleaning and Preprocessing:

Financial data often requires cleaning and preprocessing before analysis. In Jupyter Notebook, you can iteratively clean and transform your dataset, observing the effects of each operation in real-time:

```python
# Check for missing values
df.isnull().sum()

# Fill missing values
df.fillna(method='ffill', inplace=True)
```

3. Exploratory Data Analysis (EDA):

Use visualization libraries such as Matplotlib and Seaborn to explore your data and identify trends, patterns, and anomalies:

```python
import matplotlib.pyplot as plt
import seaborn as sns

# Plotting the closing prices
plt.figure(figsize=(14, 7))
sns.lineplot(data=df, x='Date', y='Close', hue='Ticker')
plt.title('Historical Stock Prices')
plt.xlabel('Date')
plt.ylabel('Closing Price')
plt.show()
```

` ` `

4. Statistical Analysis:

Perform statistical analysis directly within the notebook, leveraging libraries like SciPy and Statsmodels. For example, you can calculate the correlation between different stocks:

```python
# Calculate the correlation matrix
correlation_matrix = df.corr()
sns.heatmap(correlation_matrix,              annot=True, cmap='coolwarm')
plt.title('Correlation Matrix')
plt.show()
```

5. Building Financial Models:

Implement complex financial models such as portfolio optimization or risk assessment directly within the notebook. For instance, you can use the `yfinance` library to fetch data and perform a simple portfolio analysis:

```python
import yfinance as yf
import numpy as np

# Fetch stock data for a portfolio
tickers = ['AAPL', 'MSFT', 'GOOGL']
data    =    yf.download(tickers,    start='2020-01-01', end='2021-01-01')['Adj Close']
```

```python
# Calculate daily returns
returns = data.pct_change().dropna()

# Mean and covariance of returns
mean_returns = returns.mean()
cov_matrix = returns.cov()

# Portfolio optimization
num_portfolios = 10000
results = np.zeros((3, num_portfolios))

for i in range(num_portfolios):
    weights = np.random.random(len(tickers))
    weights /= np.sum(weights)
    portfolio_return = np.sum(mean_returns * weights) * 252
    portfolio_stddev        =        np.sqrt(np.dot(weights.T,
np.dot(cov_matrix, weights))) * np.sqrt(252)
    results[0, i] = portfolio_return
    results[1, i] = portfolio_stddev
    results[2, i] = results[0, i] / results[1, i]

# Plotting the efficient frontier
plt.scatter(results[1,   :],   results[0,   :],   c=results[2,   :],
cmap='YlGnBu', marker='o')
plt.title('Efficient Frontier')
plt.xlabel('Annualized Volatility')
plt.ylabel('Annualized Return')
plt.colorbar(label='Sharpe Ratio')
```

```
plt.show()
` ` `
```

Sharing and Collaborating with Jupyter Notebook

One of the standout features of Jupyter Notebook is its ability to facilitate collaboration. You can easily share your notebooks with colleagues, enabling them to reproduce your analysis, provide feedback, and build upon your work. Notebooks can be shared as files, exported to various formats (such as HTML and PDF), or hosted on platforms like GitHub and JupyterHub.

Jupyter Notebook is more than just an environment for writing and running code; it's a comprehensive tool that enhances every aspect of the financial analysis workflow. By integrating code, data, and visualizations into a single document, Jupyter Notebook makes it easier to perform, document, and share complex financial analyses. Embrace Jupyter Notebook, and transform the way you approach financial data analysis, making your workflow more interactive, efficient, and collaborative.

CHAPTER 2: DATA WRANGLING AND MANIPULATION TECHNIQUES

B efore we begin, it's essential to understand the basic types of join operations provided by Pandas. The library offers several methods, each tailored for specific needs:

1. Inner Join: Returns only the rows that have matching values in both datasets.

2. Outer Join: Returns all rows from both datasets, filling in `NaN` where there are missing matches.

3. Left Join: Returns all rows from the left dataset, and the matched rows from the right dataset. Rows in the left dataset without a match in the right dataset will have `NaN` values in the result.

4. Right Join: Returns all rows from the right dataset, and the matched rows from the left dataset. Rows in the right dataset without a match in the left dataset will have `NaN` values in the result.

Practical Application

Loading and Preparing Datasets

Imagine you have two datasets: one containing stock prices and another containing company earnings. First, let's load these datasets into Pandas DataFrames.

```python
import pandas as pd

# Load stock prices dataset
stock_prices = pd.read_csv('stock_prices.csv')
# Load company earnings dataset
company_earnings = pd.read_csv('company_earnings.csv')
```

```python
# Sample structure of stock_prices.csv
# Date, Ticker, Close
# 2021-01-01, AAPL, 132.69
# 2021-01-01, MSFT, 222.75

# Sample structure of company_earnings.csv
# Date, Ticker, Earnings
# 2021-01-01, AAPL, 111.44
# 2021-01-01, MSFT, 77.31
```

Merging Datasets

To merge these datasets on the `Date` and `Ticker` columns, we can use the `merge` function in Pandas. Here's how to perform different types of joins:

1. Inner Join: This join returns only the rows where there is a match in both datasets.

```python
inner_merged = pd.merge(stock_prices, company_earnings, on=['Date', 'Ticker'], how='inner')
print(inner_merged)
```

2. Outer Join: This join returns all rows from both datasets, filling in `NaN` for missing matches.

```python
outer_merged = pd.merge(stock_prices, company_earnings, on=['Date', 'Ticker'], how='outer')
print(outer_merged)
```

3. Left Join: This join returns all rows from the left dataset and matched rows from the right dataset.

```python
left_merged = pd.merge(stock_prices, company_earnings, on=['Date', 'Ticker'], how='left')
```

```python
print(left_merged)
```

4. Right Join: This join returns all rows from the right dataset and matched rows from the left dataset.

```python
right_merged = pd.merge(stock_prices, company_earnings, on=['Date', 'Ticker'], how='right')
print(right_merged)
```

Practical Example: Merging Stock Prices and Economic Indicators

For a more complex example, consider merging stock prices with economic indicators like GDP growth and interest rates. Here's how to achieve this:

```python
# Load economic indicators dataset
economic_indicators = pd.read_csv('economic_indicators.csv')

# Sample structure of economic_indicators.csv
# Date, GDP_growth, Interest_rate
# 2021-01-01, 3.2, 0.25

# Merge stock prices with economic indicators
merged_data = pd.merge(stock_prices, economic_indicators, on='Date', how='inner')
```

```python
print(merged_data)
```

Handling Duplicate Columns

When merging datasets, you might encounter columns with the same name. Pandas handles these by appending suffixes to the overlapping columns. You can specify these suffixes using the `suffixes` parameter:

```python
# Example of handling duplicate columns
merged_with_suffixes = pd.merge(stock_prices, company_earnings, on=['Date', 'Ticker'], how='inner', suffixes=('_price', '_earning'))
print(merged_with_suffixes)
```

Joining on Multiple Keys

In financial data analysis, it's common to join datasets on multiple keys. For example, joining on both `Date` and `Ticker` ensures that the data is aligned correctly.

```python
# Joining on multiple keys
multi_key_merged = pd.merge(stock_prices, company_earnings, on=['Date', 'Ticker'])
print(multi_key_merged)
```

Joining Datasets with Different Frequencies

Financial datasets often come with different frequencies (e.g., daily stock prices and quarterly earnings). To handle this, you can resample the data to a common frequency before merging.

```python
# Resample stock prices to quarterly data
stock_prices['Date'] = pd.to_datetime(stock_prices['Date'])
stock_prices.set_index('Date', inplace=True)
quarterly_stock_prices = stock_prices.resample('Q').last()

# Merge with quarterly earnings
quarterly_earnings = company_earnings.set_index('Date').resample('Q').last()
merged_quarterly_data = pd.merge(quarterly_stock_prices, quarterly_earnings, on=['Date', 'Ticker'])
print(merged_quarterly_data)
```

Case Study: Combining Historical Price Data with Financial Ratios

In this case study, we'll combine historical price data with financial ratios to perform a comprehensive analysis. Consider the following datasets:

1. Historical Prices:

```python
```

```python
# Load historical prices data
historical_prices = pd.read_csv('historical_prices.csv')
```

2. Financial Ratios:

```python
# Load financial ratios data
financial_ratios = pd.read_csv('financial_ratios.csv')
```

```python
# Sample structure of historical_prices.csv
# Date, Ticker, Close
# 2021-01-01, AAPL, 132.69
# 2021-01-01, MSFT, 222.75

# Sample structure of financial_ratios.csv
# Date, Ticker, PE_ratio, Debt_to_Equity
# 2021-01-01, AAPL, 35.57, 1.24
# 2021-01-01, MSFT, 33.15, 0.67
```

```python
# Merge historical prices with financial ratios
merged_financial_data = pd.merge(historical_prices, financial_ratios, on=['Date', 'Ticker'], how='inner')
print(merged_financial_data)
```

Understanding Concatenation and Appending

Before we delve into practical applications, let's clarify the difference between concatenation and appending:

1. Concatenation: This involves combining two or more DataFrames along a particular axis (rows or columns). It is akin to stacking datasets on top of each other or side by side.

2. Appending: This is a specific case of concatenation where we add new rows to an existing DataFrame. It's particularly useful when you're adding new data to an existing dataset.

Practical Application

Loading and Preparing Datasets

Imagine you have multiple datasets containing daily stock prices for different years. These datasets need to be concatenated to form a single DataFrame for analysis.

```python
import pandas as pd

# Load stock prices for different years
stock_prices_2020 = pd.read_csv('stock_prices_2020.csv')
stock_prices_2021 = pd.read_csv('stock_prices_2021.csv')
stock_prices_2022 = pd.read_csv('stock_prices_2022.csv')
```

```python
```

Sample structure of stock_prices_2020.csv

Date, Ticker, Close

2020-01-01, AAPL, 75.09

2020-01-01, MSFT, 160.62

` ` `

Concatenating Datasets

To concatenate these datasets along rows (i.e., combine them vertically), use the `pd.concat()` function:

` ` `python
Concatenate stock prices for multiple years

all_stock_prices   =   . pd.concat([stock_prices_2020, stock_prices_2021, stock_prices_2022], ignore_index=True)

print(all_stock_prices)

` ` `

Concatenating Along Columns

In some scenarios, you may need to concatenate datasets along columns (i.e., side by side). For instance, you might have data with different metrics for the same dates and tickers.

` ` `python
Load different metrics for the same dates and tickers

volume_data = pd.read_csv('volume_data.csv')

market_cap_data = pd.read_csv('market_cap_data.csv')

Concatenate datasets along columns

```
combined_data = pd.concat([stock_prices_2021, volume_data,
market_cap_data], axis=1)
print(combined_data)
```

Appending Data

If you have a new dataset that you need to append to
an existing DataFrame, use the `append()` method. This is
particularly useful when you receive new data periodically and
need to update your dataset.

```python
# Load new stock prices data
new_stock_prices = pd.read_csv('new_stock_prices.csv')

# Append new data to the existing DataFrame
updated_stock_prices                                    =
stock_prices_2021.append(new_stock_prices,
ignore_index=True)
print(updated_stock_prices)
```

Handling Duplicate Indices

When concatenating or appending data, it's crucial to handle
duplicate indices properly. Pandas allows you to reset indices
or set new ones to maintain data integrity.

```python
# Concatenate and reset index
```

```
all_stock_prices_reset    =    pd.concat([stock_prices_2020,
stock_prices_2021, stock_prices_2022], ignore_index=True)
print(all_stock_prices_reset)
```
` ` `

Practical Example: Concatenating Quarterly Reports

Consider concatenating quarterly reports to create an annual dataset. Assume you have separate datasets for each quarter's financial performance.

` ` `python
```
# Load quarterly financial data
q1_data = pd.read_csv('q1_data.csv')
q2_data = pd.read_csv('q2_data.csv')
q3_data = pd.read_csv('q3_data.csv')
q4_data = pd.read_csv('q4_data.csv')

# Concatenate quarterly data to form annual data
annual_data = pd.concat([q1_data, q2_data, q3_data, q4_data],
ignore_index=True)
print(annual_data)
```
` ` `

Handling Different Column Names

Occasionally, datasets might have different column names that need to be aligned before concatenation. Pandas provides the `rename()` function to standardize column names.

```python
# Assume q1_data has columns ['Date', 'Ticker', 'Revenue_Q1']
and q2_data has ['Date', 'Ticker', 'Revenue_Q2']
q1_data.rename(columns={'Revenue_Q1':          'Revenue'},
inplace=True)
q2_data.rename(columns={'Revenue_Q2':          'Revenue'},
inplace=True)

# Concatenate after renaming columns
aligned_quarters      =      pd.concat([q1_data,      q2_data],
ignore_index=True)
print(aligned_quarters)
```

Case Study: Building a Comprehensive Financial Dataset

In this case study, we'll build a comprehensive dataset that includes stock prices, volume, market capitalization, and quarterly financial metrics. Consider the following datasets:

1. Stock Prices:
   ```python
   # Load stock prices data
   stock_prices = pd.read_csv('stock_prices.csv')
   ```

2. Volume Data:
   ```python
   # Load volume data
   ```

```python
volume_data = pd.read_csv('volume_data.csv')
```

3. Market Capitalization Data:

```python
# Load market capitalization data
market_cap_data = pd.read_csv('market_cap_data.csv')
```

4. Quarterly Financial Metrics:

```python
# Load quarterly financial metrics
q1_metrics = pd.read_csv('q1_metrics.csv')
q2_metrics = pd.read_csv('q2_metrics.csv')
q3_metrics = pd.read_csv('q3_metrics.csv')
q4_metrics = pd.read_csv('q4_metrics.csv')
```

```python
# Concatenate quarterly financial metrics
quarterly_metrics = pd.concat([q1_metrics, q2_metrics, q3_metrics, q4_metrics], ignore_index=True)

# Merge stock prices with volume, market cap, and quarterly metrics
combined_financial_data = pd.concat([stock_prices, volume_data, market_cap_data, quarterly_metrics], axis=1)
print(combined_financial_data)
```

Reshaping Data: Pivoting and Unpivoting

Before diving into the practical applications, let's establish a clear understanding of these concepts:

1. Pivoting: This involves restructuring a DataFrame by converting unique values from one column into multiple columns. It essentially transforms long-form data (stacked) into wide-form data (spread out).

2. Unpivoting (Melt): This is the reverse of pivoting, where you transform wide-form data back into long-form data. This process is also known as melting.

Practical Application

Loading and Preparing Datasets

Imagine you have a dataset of monthly stock prices for several companies. This dataset will be used to demonstrate pivoting and unpivoting.

```python
import pandas as pd

# Load monthly stock prices data
data = {
    'Date': ['2021-01', '2021-01', '2021-02', '2021-02', '2021-03', '2021-03'],
    'Company': ['AAPL', 'MSFT', 'AAPL', 'MSFT', 'AAPL', 'MSFT'],
    'Price': [130, 220, 135, 225, 140, 230]
```

```
}
stock_prices = pd.DataFrame(data)
print(stock_prices)
```

```python
# Output structure
#     Date Company  Price
# 0 2021-01  AAPL   130
# 1 2021-01  MSFT   220
# 2 2021-02  AAPL   135
# 3 2021-02  MSFT   225
# 4 2021-03  AAPL   140
# 5 2021-03  MSFT   230
```

Pivoting Data

To pivot this dataset, you'll use the `pivot()` function to create a DataFrame where each company's prices become columns, and the dates remain as rows.

```python
# Pivot the dataset
pivoted_data      =      stock_prices.pivot(index='Date',
columns='Company', values='Price')
print(pivoted_data)
```

```python
# Output structure
# Company   AAPL  MSFT
# Date
# 2021-01   130   220
# 2021-02   135   225
# 2021-03   140   230
```

Unpivoting Data (Melting)

Suppose you need to revert the pivoted DataFrame back to its original long-form structure. Use the `melt()` function for this transformation.

```python
# Unpivot the dataset (melt)
unpivoted_data                                        =
pivoted_data.reset_index().melt(id_vars='Date',
value_vars=['AAPL',      'MSFT'],       var_name='Company',
value_name='Price')
print(unpivoted_data)
```

```python
# Output structure
#    Date Company  Price
# 0 2021-01  AAPL   130
```

```
# 1 2021-02  AAPL  135
# 2 2021-03  AAPL  140
# 3 2021-01  MSFT  220
# 4 2021-02  MSFT  225
# 5 2021-03  MSFT  230
` ` `
```

Handling Multi-index DataFrames

In more complex scenarios, you might deal with multi-index DataFrames. Consider the following dataset with stock prices and volumes:

```python
# Load dataset with multi-level indices
multi_index_data = {
    ('2021-01', 'AAPL'): {'Price': 130, 'Volume': 10000},
    ('2021-01', 'MSFT'): {'Price': 220, 'Volume': 15000},
    ('2021-02', 'AAPL'): {'Price': 135, 'Volume': 11000},
    ('2021-02', 'MSFT'): {'Price': 225, 'Volume': 16000},
    ('2021-03', 'AAPL'): {'Price': 140, 'Volume': 12000},
    ('2021-03', 'MSFT'): {'Price': 230, 'Volume': 17000}
}
multi_index_df = pd.DataFrame.from_dict(multi_index_data,
orient='index')
multi_index_df.index                                    =
pd.MultiIndex.from_tuples(multi_index_df.index,
names=['Date', 'Company'])
print(multi_index_df)
```

```
` ` `
```

```python
# Output structure
#          Price Volume
# Date   Company
# 2021-01 AAPL   130 10000
#     MSFT   220 15000
# 2021-02 AAPL   135 11000
#     MSFT   225 16000
# 2021-03 AAPL   140 12000
#     MSFT   230 17000
```

Pivoting Multi-index DataFrames

To pivot this multi-index DataFrame, use the `unstack()` function:

```python
# Pivot using unstack()
pivoted_multi_index                    =
multi_index_df.unstack(level='Company')
print(pivoted_multi_index)
```

```python
# Output structure
#        Price    Volume
```

```
# Company    AAPL MSFT AAPL  MSFT
# Date
# 2021-01    130 220  10000 15000
# 2021-02    135 225  11000 16000
# 2021-03    140 230  12000 17000
```

Unpivoting Multi-index DataFrames

Reverting the pivoted DataFrame back to its original form involves the `stack()` function:

```python
# Unpivot using stack()
unpivoted_multi_index                                    =
pivoted_multi_index.stack(level='Company').reset_index()
print(unpivoted_multi_index)
```

```python
# Output structure
#    Date Company Price Volume
# 0 2021-01  AAPL  130 10000
# 1 2021-01  MSFT  220 15000
# 2 2021-02  AAPL  135 11000
# 3 2021-02  MSFT  225 16000
# 4 2021-03  AAPL  140 12000
# 5 2021-03  MSFT  230 17000
```

```
```

Practical Example: Analyzing Financial Ratios

Consider a scenario where you need to analyze financial ratios for different companies. Assume you have a dataset with earnings, revenue, and profit margins for several companies across different years.

```python
# Load financial ratios data
financial_ratios_data = {
    'Year': [2020, 2020, 2021, 2021],
    'Company': ['AAPL', 'MSFT', 'AAPL', 'MSFT'],
    'Earnings': [57.41, 44.28, 60.14, 46.69],
    'Revenue': [274.52, 143.02, 294.13, 153.28],
    'Profit_Margin': [0.21, 0.31, 0.20, 0.30]
}
financial_ratios_df = pd.DataFrame(financial_ratios_data)
print(financial_ratios_df)
```

```python
# Output structure
#   Year Company Earnings Revenue Profit_Margin
# 0 2020  AAPL   57.41   274.52     0.21
# 1 2020  MSFT   44.28   143.02     0.31
# 2 2021  AAPL   60.14   294.13     0.20
# 3 2021  MSFT   46.69   153.28     0.30
```

```
```

Pivoting Financial Ratios

To pivot this dataset and compare earnings and revenue across companies, use the `pivot()` function:

```python
# Pivot the financial ratios data
pivoted_ratios = financial_ratios_df.pivot(index='Year', columns='Company', values=['Earnings', 'Revenue'])
print(pivoted_ratios)
```

```python
# Output structure
#      Earnings      Revenue
# Company  AAPL  MSFT   AAPL   MSFT
# Year
# 2020    57.41 44.28  274.52 143.02
# 2021    60.14 46.69  294.13 153.28
```

Unpivoting Financial Ratios

To analyze data in its original form or for a different perspective, unpivot the DataFrame:

```python
```

```python
# Unpivot the financial ratios data
unpivoted_ratios                                    =
pivoted_ratios.reset_index().melt(id_vars='Year',
value_vars=[('Earnings',   'AAPL'),   ('Earnings',   'MSFT'),
('Revenue', 'AAPL'), ('Revenue', 'MSFT')], var_name=['Metric',
'Company'], value_name='Value')
print(unpivoted_ratios)
```

```python
# Output structure
#   Year  Metric Company  Value
# 0 2020 Earnings   AAPL  57.41
# 1 2021 Earnings   AAPL  60.14
# 2 2020 Earnings   MSFT  44.28
# 3 2021 Earnings   MSFT  46.69
# 4 2020 Revenue   AAPL 274.52
# 5 2021 Revenue   AAPL 294.13
# 6 2020 Revenue   MSFT 143.02
# 7 2021 Revenue   MSFT 153.28
```

Mastering the techniques of pivoting and unpivoting data with Pandas empowers you to reshape your financial datasets efficiently. Whether you're converting long-form data into wide-form for easier analysis or reverting it back to its original structure, these operations provide flexibility in managing and interpreting complex datasets. As we continue our exploration of data manipulation techniques, these foundational skills will enable you to handle more sophisticated data transformations and analyses.

Hierarchical Indexing in Financial Data

Hierarchical indexing extends the capability of Pandas DataFrames by allowing you to use multiple keys (levels) to index your data. This is particularly useful in financial data analysis where you might need to slice and dice the data across various dimensions. For instance, you might want to analyze stock prices and volumes across different companies and dates simultaneously.

Hierarchical indexing can be visualized as a tree structure, where each level represents a layer of the tree. This structure enables more granular data manipulation and querying, making it easier to perform complex analyses.

Creating a Multi-Index DataFrame

Let's start by creating a multi-index DataFrame. Consider a dataset with stock prices and volumes for two companies (AAPL and MSFT) across three months (January, February, and March of 2021).

```python
import pandas as pd

# Define the data
data = {
    'Price': [130, 220, 135, 225, 140, 230],
    'Volume': [10000, 15000, 11000, 16000, 12000, 17000]
}
```

```python
# Define the multi-level index
index = pd.MultiIndex.from_tuples(
    [
        ('2021-01', 'AAPL'), ('2021-01', 'MSFT'),
        ('2021-02', 'AAPL'), ('2021-02', 'MSFT'),
        ('2021-03', 'AAPL'), ('2021-03', 'MSFT')
    ],
    names=['Date', 'Company']
)

# Create the multi-index DataFrame
multi_index_df = pd.DataFrame(data, index=index)
print(multi_index_df)
```

```python
# Output structure
#              Price  Volume
# Date    Company
# 2021-01 AAPL   130   10000
#         MSFT   220   15000
# 2021-02 AAPL   135   11000
#         MSFT   225   16000
# 2021-03 AAPL   140   12000
#         MSFT   230   17000
```

Accessing Data in a Multi-Index DataFrame

One of the key benefits of hierarchical indexing is the ability to access data at different levels of granularity. For example, you can access data for a specific date, company, or both.

```python
# Access data for a specific date
print(multi_index_df.loc['2021-01'])

# Access data for a specific company across all dates
print(multi_index_df.xs('AAPL', level='Company'))

# Access data for a specific date and company
print(multi_index_df.loc[('2021-01', 'AAPL')])
```

```python
# Output for specific date
#      Price Volume
# Company
# AAPL    130  10000
# MSFT    220  15000

# Output for specific company
#      Price Volume
# Date
# 2021-01    130  10000
```

```
# 2021-02    135  11000
# 2021-03    140  12000

# Output for specific date and company
# Price    130
# Volume  10000
# Name: (2021-01, AAPL), dtype: int64
```

Data Manipulation with Multi-Index

Hierarchical indexing not only helps in accessing data but also facilitates various data manipulation operations such as filtering, aggregating, and reshaping. Let's explore some of these operations.

Filtering Data

You can filter data based on specific conditions applied to one or more levels of the index.

```python
# Filter data for dates in 2021-02
filtered_df = multi_index_df.loc['2021-02']
print(filtered_df)
```

```python
# Output structure
#      Price  Volume
```

```
# Company
# AAPL    135  11000
# MSFT    225  16000
```

Aggregating Data

Aggregating data across different levels of the index can provide valuable insights. For instance, you can calculate the total volume of stocks traded each month.

```python
# Aggregate total volume by date
total_volume_by_date = multi_index_df.groupby(level='Date')
['Volume'].sum()
print(total_volume_by_date)
```

```python
# Output structure
# Date
# 2021-01  25000
# 2021-02  27000
# 2021-03  29000
# Name: Volume, dtype: int64
```

Reshaping Multi-Index DataFrames

Reshaping multi-index DataFrames using pivot and unstack operations can simplify complex data structures. Let's pivot the multi-index DataFrame to analyze prices and volumes side by side.

```python
# Pivot the multi-index DataFrame
pivoted_multi_index = multi_index_df.unstack(level='Company')
print(pivoted_multi_index)
```

```python
# Output structure
#        Price      Volume
# Company    AAPL MSFT   AAPL  MSFT
# Date
# 2021-01    130 220  10000 15000
# 2021-02    135 225  11000 16000
# 2021-03    140 230  12000 17000
```

Applying Functions Across Multi-Index Levels

Applying functions to data across different levels of the index can perform complex transformations. For instance, you might want to normalize volumes by dividing each value by the maximum volume for that date.

```python
# Normalize volumes by the maximum volume for each date
normalized_volume_df                          =
multi_index_df.groupby(level='Date').apply(lambda  x:  x  /
x.max())
print(normalized_volume_df)
```

```python
# Output structure
#            Price  Volume
# Date    Company
# 2021-01  AAPL  0.59091 0.66667
#      MSFT  1.00000 1.00000
# 2021-02  AAPL  0.60000 0.68750
#      MSFT  1.00000 1.00000
# 2021-03  AAPL  0.60870 0.70588
#      MSFT  1.00000 1.00000
```

Real-World Example: Sector Analysis

Consider a scenario where you need to analyze the performance of different sectors within a stock market. You have a dataset containing stock prices and volumes for various companies across different sectors and dates.

```python
```

```python
# Load sector analysis data
sector_data = {
    'Price': [130, 220, 135, 225, 140, 230, 300, 320, 310],
    'Volume': [10000, 15000, 11000, 16000, 12000, 17000,
8000, 8500, 9000],
}
sector_index = pd.MultiIndex.from_tuples(
    [
        ('2021-01', 'Tech', 'AAPL'), ('2021-01', 'Tech', 'MSFT'),
        ('2021-02', 'Tech', 'AAPL'), ('2021-02', 'Tech', 'MSFT'),
        ('2021-03', 'Tech', 'AAPL'), ('2021-03', 'Tech', 'MSFT'),
        ('2021-01', 'Finance', 'JPM'), ('2021-02', 'Finance', 'JPM'),
        ('2021-03', 'Finance', 'JPM')
    ],
    names=['Date', 'Sector', 'Company']
)

# Create the multi-index DataFrame
sector_df = pd.DataFrame(sector_data, index=sector_index)
print(sector_df)
```

```python
# Output structure
#               Price Volume
# Date   Sector Company
# 2021-01 Tech  AAPL    130 10000
#               MSFT    220 15000
```

```
# 2021-02 Tech   AAPL   135  11000
#         MSFT   225  16000
# 2021-03 Tech   AAPL   140  12000
#         MSFT   230  17000
#     Finance JPM   300  8000
# 2021-02 Finance JPM   320  8500
# 2021-03 Finance JPM   310  9000
```

Analyzing Sector Performance

You can now perform various analyses, such as calculating the average price and total volume for each sector.

```python
# Calculate average price and total volume by sector
avg_price_by_sector    =    sector_df.groupby(level='Sector')
['Price'].mean()
total_volume_by_sector = sector_df.groupby(level='Sector')
['Volume'].sum()
print(avg_price_by_sector)
print(total_volume_by_sector)
```

```python
# Output structure for average price
# Sector
# Finance  310.000000
# Tech    180.000000
```

```
# Name: Price, dtype: float64

# Output structure for total volume
# Sector
# Finance   25500
# Tech      81000
# Name: Volume, dtype: int64
` ` `
```

Hierarchical indexing in Pandas is a robust feature that allows you to manage and analyze complex financial datasets efficiently. By mastering these techniques, you can perform more granular data manipulations, access data at multiple levels of granularity, and simplify your analyses through powerful, flexible data structures. As you continue to explore data wrangling and manipulation techniques, hierarchical indexing will serve as a foundational tool for handling sophisticated financial datasets, enabling you to derive deeper insights and make more informed decisions.

Filtering and Selecting Data

Filtering data in Pandas is akin to applying a sieve, allowing only specified rows of data to pass through based on certain conditions. This process is essential for narrowing down large datasets to focus on the most relevant data points. The primary method for filtering in Pandas is through boolean indexing, which involves creating a condition that returns a boolean Series and then using this Series to filter the DataFrame.

Example: Filtering Stock Prices

Consider a DataFrame containing daily stock prices for a set of companies. You might want to filter this DataFrame to include only those days where the stock price exceeded a certain threshold.

```python
import pandas as pd

# Define the data
data = {
    'Date':    ['2021-01-01',    '2021-01-02',    '2021-01-03',
'2021-01-04'],
    'Company': ['AAPL', 'AAPL', 'MSFT', 'MSFT'],
    'Price': [130, 125, 220, 225]
}

# Create the DataFrame
df = pd.DataFrame(data)

# Convert 'Date' column to datetime
df['Date'] = pd.to_datetime(df['Date'])

# Set 'Date' as the index
df.set_index('Date', inplace=True)

# Filter the DataFrame for stock prices greater than 200
filtered_df = df[df['Price'] > 200]
print(filtered_df)
```

```python
# Output structure
#       Company  Price
# Date
# 2021-01-03  MSFT  220
# 2021-01-04  MSFT  225
```

Filtering with Multiple Conditions

Often, you'll need to apply multiple conditions to filter your data. This can be achieved using the `&` (and) and `|` (or) operators to combine conditions.

Example: Filtering by Price and Company

Let's extend the previous example to filter data where the stock price is greater than 200 and the company is 'MSFT'.

```python
# Filter the DataFrame for stock prices greater than 200 and
company 'MSFT'
filtered_df = df[(df['Price'] > 200) & (df['Company'] == 'MSFT')]
print(filtered_df)
```

```python
# Output structure
#       Company  Price
```

Date

2021-01-03 MSFT 220

2021-01-04 MSFT 225

` ` `

Selecting Specific Columns

Selecting specific columns from a DataFrame allows you to focus your analysis on pertinent metrics. This can be done using simple column indexing.

Example: Selecting the 'Price' Column

```python
# Select the 'Price' column
price_column = df['Price']
print(price_column)
```

```python
# Output structure
# Date
# 2021-01-01  130
# 2021-01-02  125
# 2021-01-03  220
# 2021-01-04  225
# Name: Price, dtype: int64
```

Advanced Selection with `.loc` and `.iloc`

Pandas provides the `.loc` and `.iloc` accessors for more advanced selection operations. The `.loc` accessor is label-based, while `.iloc` is integer-position based.

Example: Using `.loc` for Label-Based Selection

```python
# Select data for a specific date range using .loc
selected_data = df.loc['2021-01-02':'2021-01-03']
print(selected_data)
```

```python
# Output structure
#      Company Price
# Date
# 2021-01-02  AAPL  125
# 2021-01-03  MSFT  220
```

Example: Using `.iloc` for Position-Based Selection

```python
# Select the first two rows using .iloc
selected_data = df.iloc[0:2]
print(selected_data)
```

` ` `

```python
# Output structure
#       Company  Price
# Date
# 2021-01-01   AAPL   130
# 2021-01-02   AAPL   125
```
` ` `

Conditional Selection with `.query`

The `.query` method offers an elegant way to filter data based on a string expression. This method can often make your code more readable, especially when dealing with complex conditions.

Example: Filtering with `.query`

```python
# Filter data where the stock price is greater than 200
using .query
filtered_df = df.query('Price > 200')
print(filtered_df)
```
` ` `

```python
# Output structure
#       Company  Price
```

```
# Date
# 2021-01-03  MSFT  220
# 2021-01-04  MSFT  225
```
```

Real-World Application: Sector-Based Filtering

In a real-world scenario, you might have a multi-index DataFrame containing stock prices and volumes across different companies and sectors. Filtering data within such a structure can provide insights into sector performances.

# Example: Sector-Based Filtering

```python
# Define sector data
sector_data = {
    'Price': [130, 220, 135, 225, 140, 230, 300, 320, 310],
    'Volume': [10000, 15000, 11000, 16000, 12000, 17000, 8000, 8500, 9000],
}
sector_index = pd.MultiIndex.from_tuples(
    [
        ('2021-01', 'Tech', 'AAPL'), ('2021-01', 'Tech', 'MSFT'),
        ('2021-02', 'Tech', 'AAPL'), ('2021-02', 'Tech', 'MSFT'),
        ('2021-03', 'Tech', 'AAPL'), ('2021-03', 'Tech', 'MSFT'),
        ('2021-01', 'Finance', 'JPM'), ('2021-02', 'Finance', 'JPM'),
        ('2021-03', 'Finance', 'JPM')
    ],
```
```

```
    names=['Date', 'Sector', 'Company']
)

# Create the multi-index DataFrame
sector_df = pd.DataFrame(sector_data, index=sector_index)

# Filter data for Tech sector
tech_sector_df = sector_df.xs('Tech', level='Sector')
print(tech_sector_df)
```

```python
# Output structure
#               Price Volume
# Date   Company
# 2021-01 AAPL   130 10000
#     MSFT    220 15000
# 2021-02 AAPL   135 11000
#     MSFT    225 16000
# 2021-03 AAPL   140 12000
#     MSFT    230 17000
```

Applying Multiple Filters

You can apply multiple filters simultaneously to drill down into specific data subsets.

```python
```

```
# Filter Tech sector data for prices greater than 200
filtered_tech_df = tech_sector_df[tech_sector_df['Price'] > 200]
print(filtered_tech_df)
```

```python
# Output structure
#               Price Volume
# Date    Company
# 2021-01 MSFT    220  15000
# 2021-02 MSFT    225  16000
# 2021-03 MSFT    230  17000
```

Filtering and selecting data in Pandas are fundamental skills for financial analysts, enabling them to zero in on relevant information within expansive datasets. Whether using boolean indexing, conditional selection, or multi-index filtering, mastering these techniques ensures you can efficiently navigate and analyze financial data. As you continue to refine your data wrangling skills, these foundational concepts will serve as critical tools in your analytical arsenal, empowering you to extract deeper insights and make informed decisions.

Using GroupBy for Financial Data Aggregation

The `groupby` function operates through a process often referred to as "split-apply-combine." Here's a breakdown of these steps:

1. Split: The data is divided into groups based on some criteria.

2. Apply: A function is applied to each group independently.

3. Combine: The results of these operations are combined into a new DataFrame.

This mechanism is invaluable for summarizing and aggregating financial data, such as computing average stock prices, analyzing sector performance, or calculating total trading volumes.

Example: Grouping Stock Prices by Company

Consider a DataFrame containing daily stock prices for several companies.

```python
import pandas as pd

# Define the data
data = {
    'Date': ['2021-01-01', '2021-01-02', '2021-01-03', '2021-01-04', '2021-01-01', '2021-01-02', '2021-01-03', '2021-01-04'],
    'Company': ['AAPL', 'AAPL', 'AAPL', 'AAPL', 'MSFT', 'MSFT', 'MSFT', 'MSFT'],
    'Price': [130, 125, 135, 140, 220, 225, 230, 235]
}

# Create the DataFrame
df = pd.DataFrame(data)
```

```python
# Convert 'Date' column to datetime
df['Date'] = pd.to_datetime(df['Date'])

# Group by 'Company' and calculate the mean price
grouped = df.groupby('Company')['Price'].mean()
print(grouped)
```

```python
# Output structure
# Company
# AAPL   132.5
# MSFT   227.5
# Name: Price, dtype: float64
```

Aggregation Functions

Pandas provides a variety of aggregation functions, such as `mean`, `sum`, `count`, `min`, `max`, and more. You can apply these functions directly to grouped data to obtain the desired summary statistics.

Example: Calculating Total Trading Volume

Extending the previous example, let's add a trading volume column and calculate the total trading volume for each company.

```python
# Add a 'Volume' column
df['Volume'] = [10000, 15000, 20000, 25000, 30000, 35000,
40000, 45000]

# Group by 'Company' and calculate the total volume
volume_grouped = df.groupby('Company')['Volume'].sum()
print(volume_grouped)
```

```python
# Output structure
# Company
# AAPL   70000
# MSFT  150000
# Name: Volume, dtype: int64
```

Grouping by Multiple Columns

You can group data by multiple columns to perform more granular analyses. This is particularly useful in financial data when you need to consider multiple factors, such as company and date.

Example: Grouping by Company and Date

Let's compute the daily average stock price for each company.

```python
# Group by 'Company' and 'Date' and calculate the mean price
multi_grouped     =     df.groupby(['Company',     'Date'])
['Price'].mean()
print(multi_grouped)
```

```python
# Output structure
# Company  Date
# AAPL   2021-01-01   130
#      2021-01-02   125
#      2021-01-03   135
#      2021-01-04   140
# MSFT   2021-01-01   220
#      2021-01-02   225
#      2021-01-03   230
#      2021-01-04   235
# Name: Price, dtype: int64
```

Applying Custom Functions

Besides using built-in aggregation functions, you can apply custom functions to your groups using the `apply` method. This provides flexibility for more complex calculations or transformations.

Example: Custom Aggregation for Volatility

Suppose you want to calculate the daily price change percentage for each company.

```python
# Define a custom function to calculate daily price change
percentage
def price_change(group):
    group = group.sort_index()
    group['Price_Change'] = group['Price'].pct_change() * 100
    return group

# Apply the custom function to each group
price_change_grouped                                        =
df.groupby('Company').apply(price_change)
print(price_change_grouped)
```

```python
# Output (truncated for brevity)
#     Date Company Price Volume Price_Change
# 0 2021-01-01  AAPL  130 10000     NaN
# 1 2021-01-02  AAPL  125 15000  -3.846154
# 2 2021-01-03  AAPL  135 20000   8.000000
# 3 2021-01-04  AAPL  140 25000   3.703704
# 4 2021-01-01  MSFT  220 30000     NaN
# 5 2021-01-02  MSFT  225 35000   2.272727
```

```
# 6 2021-01-03   MSFT   230   40000    2.222222
# 7 2021-01-04   MSFT   235   45000    2.173913
```
` ` `

Real-World Application: Sector Analysis

In a real-world scenario, you might analyze stock performances across different sectors. This involves grouping data by sector and company, then applying aggregation functions to summarize the data.

Example: Analyzing Sector Performance

` ` `python
```python
# Define sector data
sector_data = {
    'Date':    ['2021-01-01',  '2021-01-02',  '2021-01-03',
'2021-01-04',  '2021-01-01',  '2021-01-02',  '2021-01-03',
'2021-01-04',  '2021-01-01',  '2021-01-02',  '2021-01-03',
'2021-01-04'],

    'Company': ['AAPL', 'AAPL', 'AAPL', 'AAPL', 'MSFT', 'MSFT',
'MSFT', 'MSFT', 'JPM', 'JPM', 'JPM', 'JPM'],

    'Sector': ['Tech', 'Tech', 'Tech', 'Tech', 'Tech', 'Tech', 'Tech',
'Tech', 'Finance', 'Finance', 'Finance', 'Finance'],

    'Price': [130, 125, 135, 140, 220, 225, 230, 235, 100, 105,
110, 115],

    'Volume': [10000, 15000, 20000, 25000, 30000, 35000,
40000, 45000, 20000, 25000, 30000, 35000]
}
```

Create the DataFrame
```
```

```python
sector_df = pd.DataFrame(sector_data)

# Group by 'Sector' and 'Company' and calculate the mean and
sum of prices and volumes
sector_grouped          =          sector_df.groupby(['Sector',
'Company']).agg({
    'Price': ['mean', 'sum'],
    'Volume': ['sum']
})
print(sector_grouped)
```

```python
# Output structure
#          Price      Volume
#          mean  sum    sum
# Sector Company
# Finance JPM    107.5  430  110000
# Tech   AAPL    132.5  530  70000
#        MSFT    227.5  910  150000
```

Aggregating Time Series Data

Financial data often involves time series, where you might need to aggregate data over different time periods, such as daily, weekly, or monthly.

Example: Weekly Aggregation of Stock Prices

Let's aggregate the stock prices on a weekly basis to analyze the average weekly price.

```python
# Convert 'Date' to datetime and set as index
sector_df['Date'] = pd.to_datetime(sector_df['Date'])
sector_df.set_index('Date', inplace=True)

# Resample the data on a weekly basis and calculate the mean price
weekly_grouped = sector_df.resample('W').mean()
print(weekly_grouped)
```

```python
# Output structure
#         Price     Volume
# Date
# 2021-01-03 158.333333 22500.000000
# 2021-01-10 183.333333 26666.666667
```

Utilizing the `groupby` function for data aggregation in Pandas empowers you to derive meaningful insights from financial datasets. Whether summarizing stock prices, calculating trading volumes, or analyzing sector performance, the ability to group and aggregate data is indispensable for financial analysts. By mastering these techniques, you can streamline your data analysis processes, uncover trends, and make informed, data-driven decisions. As you incorporate these concepts into your workflow, you'll find yourself better equipped to tackle the complex challenges inherent in financial data analysis.

Applying Functions to Datasets

Understanding the apply Method

The `apply` method is a versatile tool that allows you to apply a function along the axis of a DataFrame or Series. Whether you need to perform a row-wise operation, a column-wise operation, or an element-wise transformation, `apply` is your go-to method. Here's a succinct example:

```python
import pandas as pd

# Sample financial data
data = {'Symbol': ['AAPL', 'GOOGL', 'MSFT', 'AMZN'],
        'Price': [150.75, 2735.55, 299.87, 3451.50],
        'Volume': [32000000, 1500000, 23000000, 3500000]}
df = pd.DataFrame(data)

# Define a custom function to calculate the average dollar
```

volume

```python
def calc_dollar_volume(row):
    return row['Price'] * row['Volume']

# Apply the custom function to each row
df['DollarVolume'] = df.apply(calc_dollar_volume, axis=1)
print(df)
```

This snippet calculates the dollar volume for each stock by multiplying the price by the volume. The new column 'DollarVolume' is added to the DataFrame, showcasing how easily custom calculations can be integrated.

Lambda Functions for Quick Transformations

Often, you need to apply a simple transformation without the overhead of defining a full function. Lambda functions are perfect for these scenarios. Here's an example where we convert stock prices from USD to EUR, assuming a conversion rate of 1 USD = 0.85 EUR:

```python
# Apply a lambda function to convert prices to EUR
df['Price_EUR'] = df['Price'].apply(lambda x: x * 0.85)
print(df)
```

In a single line, we transformed the 'Price' column, again illustrating the brevity and power of lambda functions with `apply`.

Leveraging map and applymap for Element-wise Operations

While `apply` is powerful, sometimes more granular control is needed. The `map` and `applymap` methods cater to element-wise operations. `map` is used for Series, and `applymap` for DataFrames.

Consider a scenario where we need to flag high-volume stocks. We can use `map` for this:

```python
# Define a function to flag high-volume stocks
def flag_high_volume(volume):
    return 'High' if volume > 10000000 else 'Low'

# Apply the function to the 'Volume' column
df['Volume_Flag'] = df['Volume'].map(flag_high_volume)
print(df)
```

For DataFrame-wide operations, `applymap` comes into play. Suppose we want to format all numeric values to two decimal places:

```python
# Apply formatting to all numeric values
df = df.applymap(lambda x: f'{x:.2f}' if isinstance(x, (int, float)) else x)
print(df)
```

```
` ` `
```

This ensures a consistent presentation of numeric data across the entire DataFrame.

Aggregating Data with GroupBy and Custom Functions

The `groupby` method is indispensable for aggregating data based on categorical variables. Coupling `groupby` with custom aggregation functions enables deep analysis. Consider calculating the average dollar volume for each volume flag category:

```python
# Group by 'Volume_Flag' and calculate the mean 'DollarVolume'
average_dollar_volume    =    df.groupby('Volume_Flag')['DollarVolume'].apply(lambda x: x.mean())
print(average_dollar_volume)
```

This aggregation provides insights into how average dollar volumes differ between high- and low-volume stocks.

Transformation and Filtering with Custom Functions

Custom functions are also crucial in transforming and filtering datasets. For instance, if we need to normalize stock prices for further analysis:

```python
```

```python
# Define a normalization function
def normalize(series):
    return (series - series.min()) / (series.max() - series.min())

# Apply the normalization function to the 'Price' column
df['Normalized_Price'] = normalize(df['Price'])
print(df)
```

Normalization scales the stock prices between 0 and 1, facilitating comparisons across different stocks.

Applying Functions with Conditions

Sometimes, functions need to be applied conditionally. The `np.where` function from the NumPy library is excellent for this:

```python
import numpy as np

# Apply a conditional function to create a new column
df['Price_Category'] = np.where(df['Price'] > 1000, 'Expensive', 'Affordable')
print(df)
```

This categorizes stocks based on their price, adding another layer of analysis.

Practical Example: Calculating Moving Averages

Moving averages are a staple in financial analysis. Let's compute a 3-day moving average for stock prices:

```python
# Sample time series data
time_data = {'Symbol': ['AAPL', 'AAPL', 'AAPL', 'GOOGL', 'GOOGL', 'GOOGL'],
        'Date': ['2023-01-01', '2023-01-02', '2023-01-03', '2023-01-01', '2023-01-02', '2023-01-03'],
        'Price': [150.75, 152.00, 154.00, 2735.55, 2740.00, 2750.00]}
time_df = pd.DataFrame(time_data)
time_df['Date'] = pd.to_datetime(time_df['Date'])

# Calculate moving average for each symbol
time_df['3-Day MA'] = time_df.groupby('Symbol')['Price'].apply(lambda x: x.rolling(window=3).mean())
print(time_df)
```

This example demonstrates how to apply a custom rolling window calculation, a common requirement in time series analysis.

Mastering the application of functions to datasets in Pandas unlocks a higher dimension of data analysis and manipulation. From `apply` and `map` to `groupby` and conditional functions, the versatility and power they offer are indispensable. These techniques enable you to tailor your analyses precisely to your needs, transforming raw financial data into meaningful insights swiftly and efficiently. As you incorporate these methods into your workflow, you'll find your analytical capabilities expanding, allowing for increasingly sophisticated data interpretations and decisions.

Understanding and employing these various techniques, you'll elevate your data manipulation skills, ensuring precise, efficient, and insightful financial analyses.

Working with Date and Time Data

Pandas offers the `datetime` module and the `Timestamp` object to work with date and time data. These tools allow you to convert strings to datetime objects, manipulate date ranges, and perform arithmetic operations. The `DatetimeIndex` is another powerful feature that facilitates time-based indexing and slicing.

```python
import pandas as pd

# Sample date and time data
date_strings = ['2023-01-01', '2023-01-02', '2023-01-03']
date_times = pd.to_datetime(date_strings)
print(date_times)
```

This code converts a list of date strings into a `DatetimeIndex` object, which can be used for various time-based operations.

Creating and Indexing Time Series Data

Time series data is a sequence of data points indexed by time. Pandas allows you to create time series data easily, enabling you to analyze trends, seasonal patterns, and other temporal factors. Here's an example:

```python
# Sample financial time series data
data = {'Price': [150.75, 152.00, 154.00]}
time_series = pd.DataFrame(data, index=pd.to_datetime(['2023-01-01', '2023-01-02', '2023-01-03']))
print(time_series)
```

In this example, we create a DataFrame with prices indexed by dates, forming a time series. You can now perform various time-based operations on this DataFrame.

Resampling Time Series Data

Resampling is the process of converting a time series from one frequency to another. For instance, you might want to convert daily stock prices to monthly averages. Pandas' `resample` method makes this straightforward:

```python
# Resampling to monthly frequency
```

```python
monthly_series = time_series.resample('M').mean()
print(monthly_series)
```

This code resamples the daily time series data to a monthly frequency, calculating the mean price for each month.

Handling Time Zones

Financial data often spans multiple time zones. Pandas supports time zone-aware datetime objects, allowing you to handle and convert time zones seamlessly:

```python
# Localizing to a specific time zone
time_series.index = time_series.index.tz_localize('UTC')
print(time_series)

# Converting to another time zone
time_series = time_series.tz_convert('America/New_York')
print(time_series)
```

In this example, we localize the time series to UTC and then convert it to the New York time zone.

Time-based Indexing and Slicing

Time-based indexing and slicing are powerful features that allow you to extract specific periods from your time series data. Here's how you can do it:

```python
# Extracting data for a specific period
jan_2023 = time_series['2023-01']
print(jan_2023)

# Slicing data between two dates
jan_01_to_02 = time_series['2023-01-01':'2023-01-02']
print(jan_01_to_02)
```

This code demonstrates how to extract data for January 2023 and slice the data between January 1 and January 2, 2023.

Rolling Window Calculations

Rolling window calculations are essential for computing moving averages, rolling sums, and other statistics over a specified window. This technique is widely used in financial analysis to smooth out short-term fluctuations and highlight longer-term trends:

```python
# Calculating a 2-day moving average
time_series['2-Day MA'] = time_series['Price'].rolling(window=2).mean()
print(time_series)
```

This example calculates a 2-day moving average for the stock prices, providing insights into the trend over time.

Date Offsets and Frequency Aliases

Pandas provides a range of date offsets and frequency aliases to facilitate date manipulation. These tools allow you to shift dates, generate date ranges, and perform other date-based operations:

```python
# Creating a date range with a business day frequency
business_days = pd.date_range(start='2023-01-01', periods=5, freq='B')
print(business_days)

# Shifting dates by one month
shifted_dates = time_series.shift(1, freq='M')
print(shifted_dates)
```

In this example, we create a date range with business day frequency and shift the dates in the time series by one month.

Practical Example: Working with Market Hours

Working with market hours is a common requirement in financial analysis. Here's how you can filter data based on market hours:

```python
# Sample intraday data with market hours
intraday_data = {'Price': [150.75, 151.00, 152.50, 153.00, 154.25]}
intraday_index = pd.date_range(start='2023-01-01 09:00', periods=5, freq='H')
intraday_series = pd.DataFrame(intraday_data, index=intraday_index)
print(intraday_series)

# Filtering data for market hours (9 AM to 4 PM)
market_hours = intraday_series.between_time('09:00', '16:00')
print(market_hours)
```

This example creates an intraday time series and filters the data to include only market hours from 9 AM to 4 PM.

Mastering date and time data manipulation in Pandas is crucial for comprehensive financial analysis. Whether you're resampling data, handling time zones, performing rolling window calculations, or filtering based on market hours, Pandas provides the tools you need to handle temporal data with precision and efficiency. By incorporating these techniques into your workflow, you'll be better equipped to analyze financial trends, make informed decisions, and gain deeper insights into your data.

Creating and Modifying Columns

Adding New Columns

Creating a new column in a DataFrame is straightforward with Pandas. You can add a column by simply assigning a value or a series of values to a new column name.

Example 1: Adding a Constant Column

Let's start with a basic example of adding a constant column to a DataFrame.

```python
import pandas as pd

# Sample financial data
data = {
    'Date': ['2023-01-01', '2023-01-02', '2023-01-03'],
    'Price': [150.75, 152.00, 154.00]
}

df = pd.DataFrame(data)

# Adding a constant column
df['Volume'] = 1000
print(df)
```

In this example, we've added a new column called 'Volume' with a constant value of 1000 across all rows. This can be useful for adding metadata or supplemental information to your dataset.

Example 2: Adding a Column Based on Calculation

Often, you need to create new columns based on calculations from existing columns. Let's calculate the daily return of a stock.

```python
# Adding a column for daily returns
df['Daily Return'] = df['Price'].pct_change()
print(df)
```

Here, we use the `pct_change` method to calculate the daily return and add it as a new column to the DataFrame. This is a common operation in financial analysis to understand price movement.

Modifying Existing Columns

Modifying existing columns involves changing their values based on certain conditions or calculations. This can be achieved through vectorized operations, which are both efficient and concise.

Example 3: Modifying Values Based on a Condition

Let's modify the 'Volume' column to reflect zero volume on weekends.

```python
# Converting 'Date' to datetime
df['Date'] = pd.to_datetime(df['Date'])

# Setting volume to zero on weekends
df.loc[df['Date'].dt.dayofweek >= 5, 'Volume'] = 0
print(df)
```

In this example, we first convert the 'Date' column to datetime format. We then use the `loc` method to find rows where the day of the week is Saturday (5) or Sunday (6) and set the 'Volume' to zero for those rows. This technique is useful for cleaning and preprocessing data based on specific rules.

Creating Columns with Conditional Logic

You can create columns that depend on conditional logic using the `np.where` function from the NumPy library. This is particularly useful for categorizing data.

Example 4: Creating a Conditional Column

Let's categorize the stock price movements as 'Up' or 'Down' based on the daily returns.

```python
import numpy as np

# Creating a column for price movement direction
```

```python
df['Direction'] = np.where(df['Daily Return'] > 0, 'Up', 'Down')
print(df)
```

In this example, we use `np.where` to create a new column called 'Direction' that indicates whether the price moved up or down based on the 'Daily Return' column.

Vectorized Operations for Efficient Modifications

Pandas excels at vectorized operations, allowing you to perform computations across entire columns without loops. This enhances performance, especially when dealing with large datasets.

Example 5: Vectorized Computation of Moving Averages

Calculating moving averages is a common task in financial analysis. Let's compute a 3-day moving average for the stock prices.

```python
# Calculating a 3-day moving average
df['3-Day MA'] = df['Price'].rolling(window=3).mean()
print(df)
```

Here, we use the `rolling` method to create a rolling window of 3 days and then compute the mean within that window. The result is a new column '3-Day MA' that smooths out short-term fluctuations in stock prices.

Practical Example: Creating Technical Indicators

Technical indicators are often used in financial analysis to identify trends and signals. Let's create a new column for the Relative Strength Index (RSI), a popular momentum indicator.

```python
# Function to calculate RSI
def calculate_rsi(series, window):
    delta = series.diff()
    gain = (delta.where(delta > 0, 0)).fillna(0)
    loss = (-delta.where(delta < 0, 0)).fillna(0)
    avg_gain = gain.rolling(window=window).mean()
    avg_loss = loss.rolling(window=window).mean()
    rs = avg_gain / avg_loss
    rsi = 100 - (100 / (1 + rs))
    return rsi

# Applying RSI calculation to the DataFrame
df['RSI'] = calculate_rsi(df['Price'], window=14)
print(df)
```

In this example, we define a function to calculate the RSI based on a 14-day window. We then apply this function to the 'Price' column to create a new 'RSI' column. This technical indicator helps in identifying overbought and oversold conditions in the market.

Combining Multiple Columns

Sometimes, you need to combine multiple columns to create a new one. This can be done using vectorized operations and Pandas' `apply` method.

Example 6: Combining Columns to Calculate Weighted Average

Let's calculate a weighted average price based on volume.

```python
# Adding random volume data
df['Volume'] = [1000, 1500, 2000]

# Calculating the weighted average price
df['Weighted Avg Price'] = (df['Price'] * df['Volume']).cumsum() /
df['Volume'].cumsum()
print(df)
```

In this example, we calculate the cumulative weighted average price by multiplying the price by volume, taking the cumulative sum, and dividing by the cumulative sum of the volume. This technique is useful for understanding the average price paid for a security over time, weighted by trading volume.

Creating and modifying columns in Pandas is a fundamental skill that empowers you to tailor your financial datasets to your specific analytical needs. By mastering these techniques, you can derive new insights, clean and preprocess your data, and implement complex calculations efficiently. From adding constant columns to performing vectorized operations, these skills are essential for any financial analyst seeking to leverage the full power of Pandas.

Handling Large Datasets Efficiently

Optimizing Memory Usage

Memory optimization is crucial when working with large datasets. One effective approach is to reduce the memory footprint of your DataFrame by selecting appropriate data types for each column. Pandas provides several data types, and choosing the right one can significantly save memory.

Example 1: Using Efficient Data Types

Let's start by exploring how to use more efficient data types to reduce memory usage.

```python
import pandas as pd
import numpy as np

# Sample large dataset
data = {
    'Date': pd.date_range(start='2023-01-01', periods=100000,
freq='T'),
```

```
    'Price': np.random.uniform(100, 200, 100000),
    'Volume': np.random.randint(1, 1000, 100000)
}

df = pd.DataFrame(data)

# Checking initial memory usage
print(df.info())

# Converting data types to optimize memory usage
df['Price'] = df['Price'].astype('float32')
df['Volume'] = df['Volume'].astype('int32')

# Checking memory usage after optimization
print(df.info())
```

In this example, we create a large dataset with 100,000 rows. Initially, the 'Price' column uses the default 'float64' data type, and the 'Volume' column uses the default 'int64' data type. By converting these columns to 'float32' and 'int32' respectively, we can significantly reduce the memory usage.

Leveraging Efficient Data Structures

Pandas offers various efficient data structures that can handle large datasets more effectively. One such structure is the `Categorical` data type, which is particularly useful for columns with repeated values.

Example 2: Using Categorical Data Types

Let's see how using the `Categorical` data type can optimize memory usage for columns with repeated values.

```python
# Sample dataset with repeated values
data = {
    'Date': pd.date_range(start='2023-01-01', periods=100000, freq='T'),
    'Sector': np.random.choice(['Technology', 'Finance', 'Healthcare'], 100000)
}

df = pd.DataFrame(data)

# Checking initial memory usage
print(df.info())

# Converting 'Sector' to Categorical data type
df['Sector'] = df['Sector'].astype('category')

# Checking memory usage after optimization
print(df.info())
```

In this example, we create a dataset with a 'Sector' column containing repeated values. By converting this column to the `Categorical` data type, we can significantly reduce the memory usage because Pandas stores each unique value only once.

Performing High-Performance Computations

Vectorized operations are a powerful feature of Pandas that enable you to perform computations across entire columns without using loops. These operations are implemented in C, making them much faster than equivalent Python operations.

Example 3: Vectorized Computations for Performance

Let's calculate the exponential moving average (EMof stock prices using vectorized operations.

```python
# Function to calculate EMA
def calculate_ema(series, span):
    return series.ewm(span=span, adjust=False).mean()

# Applying EMA calculation
df['EMA'] = calculate_ema(df['Price'], span=20)
print(df)
```

In this example, we use the `ewm` method to calculate the exponential moving average of the 'Price' column. This method is highly efficient because it leverages vectorized operations.

Chunking Large Datasets

When working with datasets that are too large to fit into

memory, you can process them in chunks. This approach involves reading and processing the data in smaller portions, which reduces memory usage and improves performance.

Example 4: Reading Large Datasets in Chunks

Let's read a large CSV file in chunks and perform a simple aggregation.

```python
# Define the chunk size
chunk_size = 10000

# Initialize an empty list to store results
chunk_list = []

# Read and process data in chunks
for chunk in pd.read_csv('large_financial_data.csv', chunksize=chunk_size):
    chunk['Daily Return'] = chunk['Price'].pct_change()
    # Perform aggregation on each chunk
    chunk_agg = chunk.groupby('Sector')['Daily Return'].mean()
    chunk_list.append(chunk_agg)

# Concatenate results from all chunks
final_result = pd.concat(chunk_list)
print(final_result)
```

In this example, we read a large CSV file in chunks of 10,000 rows. For each chunk, we calculate the daily return and perform an aggregation by sector. Finally, we concatenate the results from all chunks to obtain the final aggregated result.

Parallel Processing with Dask

Dask is a parallel computing library that integrates seamlessly with Pandas. It allows you to scale your data processing tasks across multiple cores and even clusters, making it ideal for handling large datasets.

Example 5: Using Dask for Parallel Processing

Let's use Dask to perform parallel processing on a large dataset.

```python
import dask.dataframe as dd

# Load large CSV file with Dask
ddf = dd.read_csv('large_financial_data.csv')

# Perform parallel computation
ddf['Daily Return'] = ddf['Price'].pct_change()
result = ddf.groupby('Sector')['Daily Return'].mean().compute()
print(result)
```

In this example, we use Dask to read a large CSV file

and perform parallel computation. The `compute` method triggers the actual computation, leveraging multiple cores to process the data efficiently.

Using `numexpr` for Faster Computations

The `numexpr` library can significantly speed up numerical computations in Pandas by leveraging multi-threading and optimized algorithms.

Example 6: Speeding Up Computations with `numexpr`

Let's speed up a computation-heavy operation using `numexpr`.

```python
import numexpr as ne

# Sample DataFrame
df = pd.DataFrame({
    'a': np.random.randn(1000000),
    'b': np.random.randn(1000000),
    'c': np.random.randn(1000000)
})

# Perform computation using numexpr
df['d'] = ne.evaluate('a + b * c')
print(df.head())
```

In this example, we use `numexpr` to perform a computation-heavy operation involving multiplication and addition. The `ne.evaluate` function optimizes the computation, making it faster than standard Pandas operations.

Efficiently handling large datasets is a critical skill for financial analysts. By optimizing memory usage, leveraging efficient data structures, performing vectorized operations, processing data in chunks, and utilizing parallel processing with Dask and `numexpr`, you can manage and analyze large datasets effectively. These techniques empower you to extract valuable insights while maintaining performance, ensuring that you can tackle even the largest financial datasets with confidence.

CHAPTER 3: FINANCIAL DATA ANALYSIS AND VISUALIZATION

Time series data consists of observations recorded at specific time intervals. This type of data is ubiquitous in finance—whether it's stock prices, trading volumes, interest rates, or economic indicators. Each data point is associated with a timestamp, allowing analysts to track changes and trends over time.

Example: Stock Price Time Series

Consider the daily closing prices of a stock. Each day's closing price is a data point, and the sequence of these prices over days, months, or years forms a time series.

```python
import pandas as pd
```

```
# Sample time series data
data = {
    'Date':    pd.date_range(start='2023-01-01',    periods=10,
freq='D'),
    'Close': [150, 152, 153, 151, 150, 148, 149, 151, 152, 153]
}

df = pd.DataFrame(data)
df.set_index('Date', inplace=True)
print(df)
```

In this example, the `Date` column serves as the index, and the `Close` column contains the daily closing prices of the stock.

Importance of Time Series Data in Finance

Time series data is crucial for several reasons:

1. Trend Analysis: Financial analysts use time series data to identify long-term trends, which can inform investment strategies and economic forecasts.

2. Seasonality Detection: Understanding seasonal patterns —such as quarterly earnings or holiday sales—helps in predicting future performance.

3. Volatility Measurement: Time series data allows for the calculation of volatility, a key metric in risk management.

4. Correlation Analysis: Examining the correlation between different time series (e.g., stock prices and interest rates)

can uncover relationships and dependencies important for portfolio management.

Key Characteristics of Time Series Data

Time series data exhibits several key characteristics that are essential to understand:

1. Trend: A long-term increase or decrease in the data.

2. Seasonality: Regular, predictable changes that repeat over a specific period.

3. Cyclical Patterns: Irregular fluctuations often tied to economic cycles.

4. Stationarity: A time series where statistical properties like mean and variance are constant over time.

Example: Visualizing Trends and Seasonality

Let's visualize a time series to identify trends and seasonality.

```python
import matplotlib.pyplot as plt

# Sample time series with trend and seasonality
date_rng = pd.date_range(start='2023-01-01', end='2023-12-31', freq='D')
trend = np.linspace(100, 200, len(date_rng))
seasonality = 10 * np.sin(np.linspace(0, 12 * np.pi, len(date_rng))) # yearly seasonality
data = {'Date': date_rng, 'Value': trend + seasonality}
```

```
df = pd.DataFrame(data)
df.set_index('Date', inplace=True)

# Plotting the time series
df.plot()
plt.title('Time Series with Trend and Seasonality')
plt.xlabel('Date')
plt.ylabel('Value')
plt.show()
```
``` `

In this example, we generate a time series that includes both a linear trend and a sinusoidal seasonal pattern. Plotting this data helps us visualize the underlying components.

Basic Time Series Analysis with Pandas

Pandas provides robust tools for time series analysis. Some of the basic operations include:

1. Time-based Indexing: Setting a datetime index for easy slicing and aggregation.

2. Resampling: Changing the frequency of time series data (e.g., daily to monthly).

3. Rolling Windows: Applying statistical functions over a rolling time window.

Example: Resampling and Rolling Calculations
```

Let's resample our time series data to a monthly frequency and calculate a rolling mean.

```python
# Resampling to monthly frequency
monthly_df = df.resample('M').mean()
print(monthly_df)

# Calculating a rolling 7-day mean
df['7-day MA'] = df['Value'].rolling(window=7).mean()
print(df)
```

In this example, we resample the daily data to a monthly frequency, taking the average for each month. We also calculate a 7-day moving average to smooth out short-term fluctuations.

Time series data forms the backbone of financial analysis, providing insights into trends, seasonality, and volatility. Mastery of time series data analysis equips financial analysts with the tools to make informed decisions and accurate predictions. As we delve deeper into this chapter, we'll build on these foundational concepts, exploring advanced techniques and real-world applications that leverage the power of Pandas to analyze financial time series data with precision and efficiency.

Grasping the essentials of time series data, you are now prepared to explore more sophisticated methods and tools that will be covered in subsequent sections. These techniques will further refine your analytical capabilities, enabling you to extract deeper insights from your financial datasets.

Parsing Dates and Times in Pandas

Introduction to Date and Time Parsing

Parsing dates and times involves converting strings or other representations of dates and times into a `datetime` object that Pandas can understand and manipulate. This is a crucial step, as financial data often comes in various formats, and having a standardized `datetime` index is essential for time series analysis.

Example: Basic Date Parsing

Consider a CSV file containing stock prices with dates represented as strings. The goal is to convert these strings into `datetime` objects.

```python
import pandas as pd

# Sample data
data = {
    'Date': ['2023-01-01', '2023-01-02', '2023-01-03'],
    'Close': [150, 152, 153]
}
```

```
# Creating a DataFrame
df = pd.DataFrame(data)

# Parsing the 'Date' column
df['Date'] = pd.to_datetime(df['Date'])
print(df)
```

In this example, the `pd.to_datetime()` function is used to convert the `Date` column from strings to `datetime` objects, enabling Pandas to recognize and handle these dates effectively.

Handling Various Date Formats

Financial data may come in a variety of date formats, such as `YYYY-MM-DD`, `MM/DD/YYYY`, or even more complex formats involving time zones. Pandas offers flexible parsing options to handle these variations.

Example: Parsing Different Date Formats

Suppose you encounter a dataset with dates in different formats. Pandas can be instructed to parse these formats correctly.

```python
# Sample data with different date formats
data = {
    'Date': ['01/01/2023', '2023-01-02  14:30', '03-01-2023
```

```
15:45:00'],
    'Close': [150, 152, 153]
}

# Specifying the format
df = pd.DataFrame(data)
df['Date'] = pd.to_datetime(df['Date'], format='%m/%d/%Y',
errors='coerce')
print(df)

# Automatically parsing various formats
df['Date'] = pd.to_datetime(df['Date'], errors='coerce')
print(df)
` ` `
```

In this example, the `format` parameter allows us to specify a date format. The `errors='coerce'` parameter ensures that any parsing errors result in `NaT` (Not a Time) instead of raising an exception. Additionally, by omitting the `format` parameter, Pandas attempts to infer the correct format automatically.

Working with Time Zones

Time zones are an important aspect of financial data, especially when dealing with international markets. Pandas provides tools to work with time zones, ensuring that date and time data is correctly localized.

Example: Handling Time Zones

Let's consider a dataset with timestamps in different time zones.

```python
# Sample data with time zones
data = {
    'Date':    ['2023-01-01    12:00:00+00:00',    '2023-01-02
12:00:00-05:00', '2023-01-03 12:00:00+09:00'],
    'Close': [150, 152, 153]
}

# Parsing the 'Date' column
df = pd.DataFrame(data)
df['Date'] = pd.to_datetime(df['Date'])
print(df)

# Converting to a specific time zone
df['Date'] = df['Date'].dt.tz_convert('America/New_York')
print(df)
```

Here, the `pd.to_datetime()` function parses the timestamps with time zones. The `dt.tz_convert()` method converts the parsed dates to a specified time zone, ensuring consistency in the analysis.

Extracting Date Components

After parsing dates, it is often necessary to extract specific components, such as the year, month, day, or even the day of the week. Pandas offers convenient methods to perform these extractions.

Example: Extracting Date Components

Let's extract various components from a parsed datetime column.

```python
# Extracting year, month, and day
df['Year'] = df['Date'].dt.year
df['Month'] = df['Date'].dt.month
df['Day'] = df['Date'].dt.day

# Extracting the day of the week
df['DayOfWeek'] = df['Date'].dt.day_name()

print(df)
```

In this example, the `dt` accessor allows us to extract the year, month, day, and day of the week from the `Date` column.

Date Range Generation

Generating a range of dates is another common task in financial analysis. Pandas provides powerful tools to create date ranges with specific frequencies.

Example: Generating Date Ranges

Let's generate a range of dates for a specific period.

```python
# Generating a date range
date_range          =          pd.date_range(start='2023-01-01',
end='2023-12-31', freq='B')
print(date_range)
```

In this example, `pd.date_range()` generates a range of business days (excluding weekends) from January 1, 2023, to December 31, 2023. The `freq='B'` parameter specifies the frequency as business days.

Parsing dates and times efficiently is pivotal in financial data analysis. Mastering these techniques with Pandas ensures that analysts can handle temporal data with precision, enabling accurate trend analysis, forecasting, and correlation studies.

Time-Based Indexing and Slicing

Time-based indexing is the process of setting the index of a DataFrame to a time-related column, which allows for powerful time-aware operations and efficient slicing. This capability is crucial when dealing with time series data, as it enables quick lookups, slicing, and aggregations based on time intervals.

Example: Creating a Time-Based Index

Consider a DataFrame containing stock prices with

corresponding dates. We will set the `Date` column as the index.

```python
import pandas as pd

# Sample data
data = {
    'Date': ['2023-01-01', '2023-01-02', '2023-01-03'],
    'Close': [150, 152, 153]
}

# Creating a DataFrame
df = pd.DataFrame(data)

# Parsing the 'Date' column
df['Date'] = pd.to_datetime(df['Date'])

# Setting 'Date' as the index
df.set_index('Date', inplace=True)
print(df)
```

In this example, after converting the `Date` column to `datetime` objects, we use the `set_index()` method to set it as the index. This allows Pandas to recognize and handle the `Date` column efficiently for time-based operations.

Slicing Data by Date

Once the DataFrame has a time-based index, slicing data by specific dates or date ranges becomes straightforward. This is particularly useful for analyzing data over specific periods, such as daily, monthly, or quarterly intervals.

Example: Slicing by Specific Date Range

Let's slice the DataFrame to retrieve data for specific dates.

```python
# Slicing data for January 2, 2023
data_on_specific_date = df.loc['2023-01-02']
print(data_on_specific_date)

# Slicing data for a date range
data_in_date_range = df.loc['2023-01-01':'2023-01-03']
print(data_in_date_range)
```

In this example, the `loc` accessor is used to slice the data. We can specify a single date or a range of dates to retrieve the corresponding data. This functionality is invaluable for conducting period-specific analyses.

Slicing Data by Time Periods

Besides specific dates, it is often necessary to slice data by broader time periods, such as months, quarters, or years. Pandas offers convenient methods to achieve this.

Example: Slicing by Month

Consider slicing the DataFrame to focus on data from a specific month.

```python
# Creating a larger dataset for demonstration
date_rng = pd.date_range(start='2023-01-01', end='2023-12-31', freq='D')
close_prices = [150 + x for x in range(len(date_rng))]
df = pd.DataFrame({'Date': date_rng, 'Close': close_prices})
df.set_index('Date', inplace=True)

# Slicing data for January 2023
january_data = df['2023-01']
print(january_data)
```

In this example, we generate a range of dates and corresponding close prices. By setting the `Date` column as the index, we can slice the DataFrame to retrieve data for January 2023 using a simple string representation of the month.

Slicing with Partial Date Strings

Pandas allows for even more flexibility by enabling slicing with partial date strings, such as just the year, month, or day. This capability can be particularly useful when analyzing data over longer periods.

Example: Slicing with Partial Date Strings

Let's slice the DataFrame using only the year or month.

```python
# Slicing data for the year 2023
year_data = df['2023']
print(year_data)

# Slicing data for the first quarter of 2023
first_quarter_data = df['2023-01':'2023-03']
print(first_quarter_data)
```

In this example, the `loc` accessor allows us to slice the data using partial date strings. We can easily retrieve data for the entire year 2023 or for the first quarter by specifying the appropriate date range.

Resampling Time Series Data

Resampling is the process of converting a time series from one frequency to another, such as from daily to monthly. This is often required for aggregating data into larger periods for trend analysis or reporting.

Example: Resampling to Monthly Data

Consider resampling the daily data to a monthly frequency.

```python
# Resampling to monthly frequency
monthly_data = df.resample('M').mean()
print(monthly_data)
```

In this example, the `resample()` method is used to change the frequency of the time series data to monthly (`'M'`). By applying the `mean()` function, we aggregate the daily close prices into monthly averages.

Handling Missing Data in Time Series

Time series data often contain missing values, which can disrupt analysis. Pandas provides methods to handle these missing values effectively.

Example: Handling Missing Data

Let's introduce some missing values and handle them.

```python
import numpy as np

# Introducing missing values
df.iloc[10:15] = np.nan

# Forward fill to handle missing values
df_filled = df.ffill()
```

```
print(df_filled)

# Backward fill to handle missing values
df_filled = df.bfill()
print(df_filled)
` ` `
```

In this example, we introduce `NaN` values into the DataFrame. The `ffill()` method fills missing values forward, while the `bfill()` method fills missing values backward, ensuring continuity in the time series data.

Mastering time-based indexing and slicing is indispensable for financial analysts working with temporal data. These techniques enable efficient data retrieval, manipulation, and aggregation, providing the foundation for advanced time series analysis. By leveraging these capabilities, you can enhance your ability to uncover trends, forecast future values, and drive strategic financial decisions. As you continue through this book, the skills learned here will be applied in more complex scenarios, solidifying your expertise in financial data analysis with Pandas.

With these techniques under your belt, you're well-equipped to handle the temporal intricacies of financial data. Continue exploring and applying these methods to unlock deeper insights and drive more informed decisions in your financial analyses.

Introduction to Resampling

Resampling is the process of converting a time series to a different frequency by either aggregating or downsampling the data. Aggregation typically involves calculating summary statistics like mean, sum, or count over the new frequency intervals. Conversely, downsampling reduces the data frequency, which can help in simplifying the dataset for specific types of analysis.

Example: Setting Up the Data

Consider a DataFrame containing minute-by-minute stock prices. We'll set the `DateTime` column as the index to facilitate time-based operations.

```python
import pandas as pd
import numpy as np

# Generating sample data
date_rng = pd.date_range(start='2023-01-01', end='2023-01-10', freq='T')
stock_prices = np.random.randn(len(date_rng)) * 10 + 100

# Creating DataFrame
df = pd.DataFrame({'DateTime': date_rng, 'Price': stock_prices})
df.set_index('DateTime', inplace=True)

print(df.head())
```

In this example, we first generate a range of dates and corresponding stock prices for each minute in a 10-day period. By setting the `DateTime` column as the index, we enable efficient time-based operations.

Resampling to a Daily Frequency

One common use case is to resample minute-by-minute data to a daily frequency, which can simplify analysis and visualization.

Example: Daily Resampling with Mean

Let's resample the time series to a daily frequency and calculate the daily mean price.

```python
# Resampling to daily frequency and calculating mean
daily_mean = df.resample('D').mean()
print(daily_mean.head())
```

In this example, the `resample()` method is used with the `'D'` frequency parameter to resample the data to daily intervals. The `mean()` function is then applied to calculate the average stock price for each day.

Resampling to a Monthly Frequency

Resampling to a monthly frequency can be useful for long-term trend analysis. This is especially relevant in financial reports and performance summaries.

Example: Monthly Resampling with Sum

Consider resampling the data to a monthly frequency and calculating the total price (sum).

```python
# Resampling to monthly frequency and calculating sum
monthly_sum = df.resample('M').sum()
print(monthly_sum.head())
```

In this example, we change the frequency to monthly using `'M'` and apply the `sum()` function to get the total stock price for each month.

Handling Missing Data During Resampling

When resampling, it's crucial to handle missing data appropriately to ensure the accuracy of the results. Pandas offers several methods for dealing with missing values during resampling, such as forward fill (`ffill`) and backward fill (`bfill`).

Example: Handling Missing Data

Let's assume there are missing values in the dataset and handle them during the resampling process.

```python
# Introducing missing values
df.iloc[1000:1050] = np.nan
```

```
# Forward fill to handle missing values
resampled_filled = df.resample('D').ffill()
print(resampled_filled.head())
```

In this example, we introduce `NaN` values into the DataFrame. By applying the `ffill()` method during resampling, we ensure that the missing values are filled forward from the last known value.

Upsampling Data

While resampling usually involves aggregating data to a lower frequency, there are cases where upsampling to a higher frequency is necessary. Upsampling, combined with interpolation, can fill in the gaps and create a more granular dataset.

Example: Upsampling with Interpolation

Consider upsampling daily data back to minute-by-minute data with interpolation.

```python
# Upsampling to minute-by-minute frequency
upsampled = df.resample('T').asfreq()

# Interpolating missing values
interpolated = upsampled.interpolate(method='linear')
print(interpolated.head())
```

` ` `

In this example, we first upsample the data to minute intervals using `asfreq()`, which introduces `NaN` values for the new frequency. We then use `interpolate()` with linear interpolation to fill in the missing values, creating a smooth transition between data points.

Applying Custom Functions During Resampling

Pandas allows for applying custom functions during the resampling process, providing the flexibility to perform more complex operations based on specific analytical needs.

Example: Custom Aggregation Function

Let's apply a custom function to calculate the range (max - min) of prices for each resampled period.

```python
# Custom aggregation function to calculate range
def price_range(x):
    return x.max() - x.min()


# Resampling to daily frequency and applying custom function
daily_range = df.resample('D').apply(price_range)
print(daily_range.head())
```

In this example, we define a custom function `price_range`

that calculates the difference between the maximum and minimum prices. We then apply this function to the resampled data to get the daily price range.

Combining Resampling with Rolling Window Calculations

Combining resampling with rolling window calculations can provide deeper insights into trends and volatility over different periods.

Example: Resampling and Rolling Mean

Consider combining resampling with a rolling mean to smooth daily data further.

```python
# Resampling to daily frequency and calculating rolling mean over 7 days
resampled_daily = df.resample('D').mean()
rolling_mean = resampled_daily.rolling(window=7).mean()
print(rolling_mean.head(14))
```

In this example, we first resample the data to daily frequency and then apply a rolling mean with a 7-day window to smooth the data further, revealing underlying trends over a week.

Resampling time series data is a powerful technique in financial data analysis, enabling analysts to aggregate or downsample data to various frequencies, handle missing values, and apply custom functions. By mastering these techniques, you can transform raw time series data into meaningful insights, driving more informed and strategic financial decisions. As you progress through this book, you'll continue to build on these foundational skills, applying them in more complex and nuanced scenarios to unlock deeper insights and enhance your financial analysis capabilities.

With these resampling techniques, you are now equipped to handle time series data efficiently and effectively, paving the way for more sophisticated analyses and improved decision-making processes in your financial endeavors.

Plotting Time Series Data

In the realm of financial analysis, visual representation of time series data is crucial. It not only provides an intuitive understanding of trends and patterns but also helps in uncovering insights that might otherwise remain hidden in raw data. Let's delve into the mechanics of plotting time series data using Pandas, ensuring you have the tools to transform raw data into meaningful visualizations.

Understanding Time Series Data

Time series data in finance typically includes historical prices of stocks, exchange rates, interest rates, or economic indicators. These datasets consist of sequential data points, typically indexed by time (e.g., daily closing prices of a stock). Analyzing and visualizing these data points over time can reveal trends, seasonality, and anomalies.

Setting Up Your Environment

Before diving in, ensure you have the necessary libraries installed. Pandas, Matplotlib, and Seaborn are essential for plotting and visualizing data. If you haven't installed them yet, you can do so using pip:

```python
!pip install pandas matplotlib seaborn
```

Let's import these libraries and set up our environment:

```python
import pandas as pd
import matplotlib.pyplot as plt
import seaborn as sns

# Optional: Set up a Seaborn style for better aesthetics
sns.set(style="darkgrid")
```

Loading and Preparing Data

For our examples, we'll use a dataset containing historical stock prices. You can download such datasets from financial websites like Yahoo Finance or use an existing CSV file. Here's how you can load and prepare your data:

```python
# Load the dataset
```

```
url = 'https://path-to-your-dataset.csv'
df = pd.read_csv(url, parse_dates=['Date'], index_col='Date')

# Display the first few rows of the DataFrame
print(df.head())
```

Ensure your dataset has a 'Date' column, which will be used as the index for time series analysis.

Basic Time Series Plot

Let's start with a simple line plot to visualize the closing prices of a stock over time:

```python
# Plotting the closing prices
plt.figure(figsize=(10, 6))
plt.plot(df['Close'], label='Closing Price')

# Adding title and labels
plt.title('Stock Closing Prices Over Time')
plt.xlabel('Date')
plt.ylabel('Closing Price')
plt.legend()
plt.show()
```

This basic plot provides a clear visual representation of the stock's performance over the specified period.

Adding Moving Averages

Moving averages help smooth out short-term fluctuations and highlight longer-term trends or cycles. Here's how to add a 50-day and a 200-day moving average to our plot:

```python
# Calculating moving averages
df['50_MA'] = df['Close'].rolling(window=50).mean()
df['200_MA'] = df['Close'].rolling(window=200).mean()

# Plotting the closing prices along with moving averages
plt.figure(figsize=(10, 6))
plt.plot(df['Close'], label='Closing Price')
plt.plot(df['50_MA'], label='50-Day Moving Average')
plt.plot(df['200_MA'], label='200-Day Moving Average')

# Adding title and labels
plt.title('Stock Closing Prices with Moving Averages')
plt.xlabel('Date')
plt.ylabel('Price')
plt.legend()
plt.show()
```

Highlighting Key Events

Sometimes, marking key events on your time series plot can provide additional context. For example, highlighting significant dates such as earnings announcements or geopolitical events can be insightful:

```python
# List of significant dates
significant_dates = ['2020-03-20', '2020-06-15']

# Plotting with significant dates highlighted
plt.figure(figsize=(10, 6))
plt.plot(df['Close'], label='Closing Price')

# Highlighting significant dates
for date in significant_dates:
    plt.axvline(pd.to_datetime(date), color='red', linestyle='--', lw=1)

# Adding title and labels
plt.title('Stock Closing Prices with Key Events Highlighted')
plt.xlabel('Date')
plt.ylabel('Price')
plt.legend()
plt.show()
```

Creating Subplots for Multiple Stocks

Visualizing multiple stocks in a single figure can be useful for comparison. Here's how you can create subplots:

```python
# Assuming df contains data for multiple stocks with columns
'Stock_A_Close', 'Stock_B_Close', etc.
stocks = ['Stock_A_Close', 'Stock_B_Close']

# Creating subplots
fig, axes = plt.subplots(nrows=len(stocks), ncols=1,
figsize=(10, 12), sharex=True)

for ax, stock in zip(axes, stocks):
    df[stock].plot(ax=ax)
    ax.set_ylabel('Price')
    ax.set_title(f'{stock} Closing Prices')

# Common x-axis label
plt.xlabel('Date')
plt.show()
```

Enhancing Plots with Seaborn

Seaborn provides additional functionality for more sophisticated visualizations. Here's an example of a line plot using Seaborn:

```python
# Using Seaborn to plot time series data
plt.figure(figsize=(10, 6))
```

```python
sns.lineplot(data=df['Close'], label='Closing Price')

# Adding title and labels
plt.title('Stock Closing Prices Over Time (Seaborn)')
plt.xlabel('Date')
plt.ylabel('Closing Price')
plt.legend()
plt.show()
```

Interactive Plots with Plotly

For interactive visualizations, Plotly is a powerful tool. Here's a basic example:

```python
import plotly.express as px

# Creating an interactive plot with Plotly
fig = px.line(df, x=df.index, y='Close', title='Interactive Stock Closing Prices')
fig.show()
```

Plotting time series data effectively can transform your financial analysis by revealing trends, patterns, and insights that are not immediately apparent in raw datasets. By leveraging the power of Pandas, Matplotlib, Seaborn, and Plotly, you can create detailed and informative visualizations that enhance your understanding and communication of financial data.

Advanced Visualization with Seaborn and Matplotlib

Setting Up Your Environment

Before we begin, make sure you have the necessary libraries installed. You can install Seaborn and Matplotlib using pip if you haven't already:

```python
!pip install seaborn matplotlib
```

Once installed, let's import these libraries and set up our environment:

```python
import pandas as pd
import matplotlib.pyplot as plt
import seaborn as sns

# Set Seaborn style for aesthetics
sns.set(style="whitegrid")
```

Loading Financial Data

For our examples, we will use a dataset containing historical stock prices. You can download such datasets from financial websites like Yahoo Finance or use an existing CSV file. Here's how to load and prepare your data:

```python
# Load the dataset
url = 'https://path-to-your-dataset.csv'
df = pd.read_csv(url, parse_dates=['Date'], index_col='Date')

# Display the first few rows of the DataFrame
print(df.head())
```

Ensure your dataset has a 'Date' column, which will be used as the index for time series analysis.

Customizing Line Plots with Seaborn

Seaborn's line plot function is a versatile tool for creating elegant and informative time series visualizations. Let's start by plotting the closing prices with added enhancements:

```python
# Plotting closing prices using Seaborn
plt.figure(figsize=(12, 6))
sns.lineplot(x=df.index, y='Close', data=df, label='Closing Price')

# Adding titles and labels
plt.title('Stock Closing Prices Over Time', fontsize=16)
```

```python
plt.xlabel('Date', fontsize=14)
plt.ylabel('Closing Price', fontsize=14)
plt.legend()
plt.show()
```

Enhancing Visuals with Annotations

Adding annotations to your plots can provide context and highlight important data points or events. Here's how you can annotate significant peaks and troughs in your data:

```python
# Finding significant peaks and troughs
peak = df['Close'].idxmax()
trough = df['Close'].idxmin()

# Plotting with annotations
plt.figure(figsize=(12, 6))
sns.lineplot(x=df.index, y='Close', data=df, label='Closing Price')
plt.axvline(peak, color='r', linestyle='--')
plt.axvline(trough, color='b', linestyle='--')

# Adding text annotations
plt.text(peak, df['Close'].max(), 'Peak', horizontalalignment='right', color='red')
plt.text(trough, df['Close'].min(), 'Trough', horizontalalignment='right', color='blue')
```

```python
# Adding titles and labels
plt.title('Stock Closing Prices with Annotations', fontsize=16)
plt.xlabel('Date', fontsize=14)
plt.ylabel('Closing Price', fontsize=14)
plt.legend()
plt.show()
```

Visualizing Distribution with Seaborn

Understanding the distribution of your financial data is essential for risk management and statistical analysis. Seaborn provides powerful functions for visualizing distributions, such as histograms and KDE plots:

```python
# Plotting distribution of closing prices
plt.figure(figsize=(12, 6))
sns.histplot(df['Close'], kde=True, bins=30, color='purple')

# Adding titles and labels
plt.title('Distribution of Closing Prices', fontsize=16)
plt.xlabel('Closing Price', fontsize=14)
plt.ylabel('Frequency', fontsize=14)
plt.show()
```

Combining Multiple Plots with Matplotlib

Creating multi-faceted visualizations can provide a comprehensive view of your data. Matplotlib allows you to combine multiple plots in a single figure using subplots:

```python
# Creating subplots
fig, (ax1, ax2) = plt.subplots(2, 1, figsize=(12, 12))

# Line plot on the first subplot
sns.lineplot(x=df.index, y='Close', data=df, ax=ax1, label='Closing Price')
ax1.set_title('Stock Closing Prices Over Time', fontsize=16)
ax1.set_xlabel('Date', fontsize=14)
ax1.set_ylabel('Closing Price', fontsize=14)

# Distribution plot on the second subplot
sns.histplot(df['Close'], kde=True, bins=30, color='purple', ax=ax2)
ax2.set_title('Distribution of Closing Prices', fontsize=16)
ax2.set_xlabel('Closing Price', fontsize=14)
ax2.set_ylabel('Frequency', fontsize=14)

# Adjusting layout
plt.tight_layout()
plt.show()
```

Creating Heatmaps for Correlation Analysis

Heatmaps are an excellent way to visualize correlations between different financial instruments or indicators. Using Seaborn, you can create heatmaps to uncover relationships within your dataset:

```python
# Calculating the correlation matrix
correlation_matrix = df.corr()

# Plotting the heatmap
plt.figure(figsize=(12, 10))
sns.heatmap(correlation_matrix,                    annot=True,
cmap='coolwarm', linewidths=0.5)

# Adding titles and labels
plt.title('Correlation Matrix of Financial Data', fontsize=16)
plt.show()
```

Advanced Time Series Plots with Seaborn

When dealing with time series data, combining line plots with additional features can provide deeper insights. Here's an example of plotting stock returns with a confidence interval:

```python
# Calculating daily returns
df['Daily Return'] = df['Close'].pct_change()
```

```python
# Plotting daily returns with confidence interval
plt.figure(figsize=(12, 6))

sns.lineplot(x=df.index, y='Daily Return', data=df, ci=95, label='Daily Return')

# Adding titles and labels
plt.title('Daily Stock Returns with 95% Confidence Interval', fontsize=16)

plt.xlabel('Date', fontsize=14)

plt.ylabel('Daily Return', fontsize=14)

plt.legend()

plt.show()
```

Combining Seaborn and Matplotlib for Enhanced Visuals

Leveraging both Seaborn and Matplotlib together can produce visually appealing and highly informative plots. Here's an example combining the two libraries to plot multiple moving averages along with daily returns:

```python
# Calculating moving averages
df['50_MA'] = df['Close'].rolling(window=50).mean()
df['200_MA'] = df['Close'].rolling(window=200).mean()

# Creating a dual-axis plot
fig, ax1 = plt.subplots(figsize=(12, 6))
```

```
# Plotting closing prices and moving averages on the first y-axis
sns.lineplot(x=df.index, y='Close', data=df, ax=ax1, label='Closing Price')
sns.lineplot(x=df.index, y='50_MA', data=df, ax=ax1, label='50-Day MA')
sns.lineplot(x=df.index, y='200_MA', data=df, ax=ax1, label='200-Day MA')
ax1.set_xlabel('Date', fontsize=14)
ax1.set_ylabel('Price', fontsize=14)
ax1.set_title('Stock Prices with Moving Averages and Daily Returns', fontsize=16)

# Creating a second y-axis for daily returns
ax2 = ax1.twinx()
sns.lineplot(x=df.index, y='Daily Return', data=df, ax=ax2, color='grey', label='Daily Return', alpha=0.5)
ax2.set_ylabel('Daily Return', fontsize=14)

# Adding legends
ax1.legend(loc='upper left')
ax2.legend(loc='upper right')
plt.show()
```

Advanced visualization with Seaborn and Matplotlib empowers you to create detailed, informative, and aesthetically pleasing charts that enhance your financial analysis. By mastering these techniques, you can communicate complex data more effectively, uncover insights, and make informed decisions with confidence.

Candlestick and OHLC Charts

Candlestick charts are renowned for their ability to depict the open, high, low, and close prices of a security over a specific period. Each "candlestick" represents a single time period, where the body of the candlestick shows the range between the opening and closing prices, and the wicks (shadows) indicate the high and low prices. This technique, originating from Japanese rice traders, remains essential for modern traders and analysts.

Setting Up Your Environment

Before we get started, ensure you have the necessary libraries installed. We will be using Matplotlib for basic charting and Plotly for interactive visualizations:

```python
!pip install matplotlib plotly
```

Once installed, import the required libraries:

```python
import pandas as pd
import matplotlib.pyplot as plt
from mplfinance.original_flavor import candlestick_ohlc
import matplotlib.dates as mdates
```

```python
import plotly.graph_objects as go
```
` ` `

Loading Financial Data

We will use historical stock data for our examples. You can source this data from various financial websites such as Yahoo Finance. Here's how to load a dataset and prepare it for visualization:

` ` `python
```python
# Load the dataset
url = 'https://path-to-your-dataset.csv'
df = pd.read_csv(url, parse_dates=['Date'], index_col='Date')

# Ensure the dataset contains the necessary columns: 'Open',
'High', 'Low', 'Close'
print(df.head())
```
` ` `

Creating Candlestick Charts with Matplotlib

Matplotlib's `mplfinance` module (previously known as `mpl_finance`) simplifies the creation of candlestick charts. Follow these steps to create a basic candlestick chart:

1. Prepare the Data: Convert the date index to Matplotlib's date format and create an OHLC array.

` ` `python
```python
df['Date'] = mdates.date2num(df.index.to_pydatetime())
```

```python
ohlc = df[['Date', 'Open', 'High', 'Low', 'Close']].copy()
```
```

2. Plot the Candlestick Chart:

```python
fig, ax = plt.subplots(figsize=(12, 6))

# Plot the candlestick chart
candlestick_ohlc(ax, ohlc.values, width=0.6, colorup='g', colordown='r')

# Format the x-axis with dates
ax.xaxis_date()
ax.xaxis.set_major_formatter(mdates.DateFormatter('%Y-%m-%d'))

# Adding titles and labels
plt.title('Candlestick Chart')
plt.xlabel('Date')
plt.ylabel('Price')
plt.grid(True)
plt.show()
```

Enhancing Candlestick Charts with Plotly

While Matplotlib provides robust plotting capabilities, Plotly offers interactive features that can greatly enhance your analysis. Let's create an interactive candlestick chart using
```

Plotly:

1. Prepare the Data:

```python
# Ensure the index is a DatetimeIndex
df.reset_index(inplace=True)
```

2. Plot the Candlestick Chart:

```python
fig = go.Figure(data=[go.Candlestick(x=df['Date'],
                    open=df['Open'],
                    high=df['High'],
                    low=df['Low'],
                    close=df['Close'])])

# Adding titles and layout options
fig.update_layout(title='Interactive Candlestick Chart',
        xaxis_title='Date',
        yaxis_title='Price',
        xaxis_rangeslider_visible=False)

fig.show()
```

Understanding OHLC Charts

OHLC charts are similar to candlestick charts but use bars instead of candles to represent price movements. They provide the same information: open, high, low, and close prices, with bars extending from the low to the high price and ticks on the left and right indicating the open and close prices.

Creating OHLC Charts with Matplotlib

Creating an OHLC chart follows a similar process to candlesticks. Here's how you can do it:

1. Prepare the data:

```python
# Convert the date index to Matplotlib's date format if not already done
if 'Date' not in df.columns:
    df['Date'] = mdates.date2num(df.index.to_pydatetime())
```

2. Plot the OHLC Chart:

```python
fig, ax = plt.subplots(figsize=(12, 6))

# Adjust the width for OHLC bars
width = 0.4

# Plot the bars
for i in range(len(df)):
```

```
    if df['Close'][i] >= df['Open'][i]:
        color = 'g'
        lower = df['Open'][i]
        height = df['Close'][i] - df['Open'][i]
    else:
        color = 'r'
        lower = df['Close'][i]
        height = df['Open'][i] - df['Close'][i]

    # Draw the line for high and low
    ax.plot([df['Date'][i], df['Date'][i]], [df['Low'][i], df['High'][i]], color='black')
    # Draw the bar for open to close
    ax.add_patch(plt.Rectangle((df['Date'][i] - width/2, lower), width, height, facecolor=color))

# Formatting the x-axis with dates
ax.xaxis_date()
ax.xaxis.set_major_formatter(mdates.DateFormatter('%Y-%m-%d'))

# Adding titles and labels
plt.title('OHLC Chart')
plt.xlabel('Date')
plt.ylabel('Price')
plt.grid(True)
plt.show()
```
```
```

Combining Candlestick and OHLC Charts with Plotly

For a comprehensive analysis, you might want to create charts that combine candlesticks with other technical indicators. Here's an example of plotting a candlestick chart alongside a moving average to identify trends:

1. Calculate the Moving Average:

```python
df['Moving_Avg'] = df['Close'].rolling(window=20).mean()
```

2. Plot the Candlestick Chart with Moving Average:

```python
fig = go.Figure()

# Adding candlestick chart
fig.add_trace(go.Candlestick(x=df['Date'],
                open=df['Open'],
                high=df['High'],
                low=df['Low'],
                close=df['Close'],
                name='Candlestick'))

# Adding moving average
fig.add_trace(go.Scatter(x=df['Date'], y=df['Moving_Avg'],
                mode='lines',    name='20-Day    Moving
```

Average'))

```
# Adding titles and layout options
fig.update_layout(title='Candlestick Chart with Moving Average',
                  xaxis_title='Date',
                  yaxis_title='Price')

fig.show()
```

Mastering candlestick and OHLC charts equips you with the ability to visualize and interpret complex price movements succinctly. These charting techniques offer a window into market sentiment, enabling timely and informed decisions. As you advance in your analytical journey, integrating these visual tools will enhance your ability to uncover trends, validate strategies, and communicate insights effectively.

Plotting Moving Averages and Bollinger Bands

Understanding Moving Averages

Moving averages are a type of smoothing technique used to reduce noise and highlight trends in financial data. There are several types of moving averages, with the Simple Moving Average (SMand the Exponential Moving Average (EMbeing the most commonly used.

- Simple Moving Average (SMA): The SMA is calculated by taking the arithmetic mean of a given set of prices over a specific number of periods. It's straightforward and effective for identifying the direction of an asset's trend.

- Exponential Moving Average (EMA): The EMA gives more weight to recent prices, making it more responsive to new information compared to the SMA. This characteristic makes EMA a preferred tool for detecting potential reversals.

Setting Up Your Environment

Ensure you have the necessary libraries installed. We will use Pandas for data manipulation and Plotly for visualization:

```python
!pip install pandas plotly
```

Import the required libraries:

```python
import pandas as pd
import plotly.graph_objects as go
```

Loading Financial Data

We will use historical stock data for our examples. Assume you have a CSV file with columns: 'Date', 'Open', 'High', 'Low', 'Close',

'Volume'. Here's how to load and prepare the dataset:

```python
# Load the dataset
url = 'https://path-to-your-dataset.csv'
df = pd.read_csv(url, parse_dates=['Date'], index_col='Date')

# Ensure the dataset contains the necessary columns: 'Open',
'High', 'Low', 'Close'
print(df.head())
```

Calculating Moving Averages

1. Simple Moving Average (SMA):

```python
# Calculate the 20-day Simple Moving Average (SMA)
df['SMA_20'] = df['Close'].rolling(window=20).mean()
```

2. Exponential Moving Average (EMA):

```python
# Calculate the 20-day Exponential Moving Average (EMA)
df['EMA_20'] = df['Close'].ewm(span=20, adjust=False).mean()
```

Plotting Moving Averages with Plotly

Now, let's plot the moving averages alongside the historical price data using Plotly:

1. Plot the Moving Averages:

```python
fig = go.Figure()

# Adding close price line
fig.add_trace(go.Scatter(x=df.index, y=df['Close'],
                mode='lines', name='Close Price'))

# Adding SMA line
fig.add_trace(go.Scatter(x=df.index, y=df['SMA_20'],
                mode='lines', name='20-Day SMA'))

# Adding EMA line
fig.add_trace(go.Scatter(x=df.index, y=df['EMA_20'],
                mode='lines', name='20-Day EMA'))

# Adding titles and layout options
fig.update_layout(title='Stock Price with 20-Day Moving Averages',
                xaxis_title='Date',
                yaxis_title='Price',
                xaxis_rangeslider_visible=False)
```

```
fig.show()
```
` ` `

Understanding Bollinger Bands

Bollinger Bands combine a moving average with two standard deviation lines plotted above and below the moving average. They are used to measure market volatility and identify overbought or oversold conditions.

- Upper Bollinger Band: The upper band is calculated by adding two standard deviations to the moving average.

- Lower Bollinger Band: The lower band is calculated by subtracting two standard deviations from the moving average.

Calculating Bollinger Bands

1. Calculate the Moving Average and Standard Deviation:

```python
# Calculate the 20-day Simple Moving Average (SMA)
df['SMA_20'] = df['Close'].rolling(window=20).mean()

# Calculate the rolling standard deviation
df['STD_20'] = df['Close'].rolling(window=20).std()
```

2. Calculate the Bollinger Bands:

```python
```

```python
# Calculate the Upper Bollinger Band
df['Upper_Band'] = df['SMA_20'] + (df['STD_20'] * 2)

# Calculate the Lower Bollinger Band
df['Lower_Band'] = df['SMA_20'] - (df['STD_20'] * 2)
```

Plotting Bollinger Bands with Plotly

1. Plot the Bollinger Bands:

```python
fig = go.Figure()

# Adding close price line
fig.add_trace(go.Scatter(x=df.index, y=df['Close'],
                mode='lines', name='Close Price'))

# Adding SMA line
fig.add_trace(go.Scatter(x=df.index, y=df['SMA_20'],
                mode='lines', name='20-Day SMA'))

# Adding upper Bollinger Band
fig.add_trace(go.Scatter(x=df.index, y=df['Upper_Band'],
                mode='lines',    name='Upper    Band',
line=dict(color='rgba(0,100,80,0.2)')))

# Adding lower Bollinger Band
fig.add_trace(go.Scatter(x=df.index, y=df['Lower_Band'],
```

```
                mode='lines',      name='Lower      Band',
line=dict(color='rgba(0,100,80,0.2)')))

    # Adding titles and layout options
    fig.update_layout(title='Bollinger Bands',
                xaxis_title='Date',
                yaxis_title='Price',
                xaxis_rangeslider_visible=False)

    fig.show()
    ` ` `
```

Practical Applications

Identifying Trends and Reversals

Moving averages and Bollinger Bands are vital for identifying market trends and potential reversals. When the price crosses above the moving average, it may indicate the beginning of an uptrend, while crossing below suggests a downtrend. Bollinger Bands help identify overbought and oversold conditions, providing trading signals. For instance, when prices touch or move outside the upper band, it might suggest overbought conditions, whereas touching the lower band could indicate oversold conditions.

Combining Indicators for Robust Analysis

Using moving averages in conjunction with Bollinger Bands provides a more comprehensive analysis. Moving averages can confirm the trend direction, while Bollinger Bands can signal potential corrections or reversals. This dual approach enhances your ability to make informed trading decisions.

Mastering the plotting of moving averages and Bollinger Bands equips you with powerful tools for analyzing financial markets. These indicators help smooth out price data, identify trends, measure volatility, and signal potential buy or sell opportunities. Integrating these techniques into your analytical toolkit will enhance your ability to interpret market dynamics and make informed decisions, ultimately advancing your expertise in financial data analysis.

Visualizing Correlations in Financial Data

Understanding Correlation

Correlation measures the strength and direction of a linear relationship between two variables. In finance, it indicates how one financial instrument's price movement is related to another's. The correlation coefficient ranges from -1 to 1:

- 1 implies a perfect positive relationship, where assets move in the same direction.

- -1 implies a perfect negative relationship, where assets move in opposite directions.

- 0 implies no linear relationship between the assets.

Setting Up the Environment

Ensure you have the necessary libraries installed. We will use

Pandas for data manipulation and Seaborn for visualization:

```python
!pip install pandas seaborn
```

Import the required libraries:

```python
import pandas as pd
import seaborn as sns
import matplotlib.pyplot as plt
```

Loading Financial Data

For this example, assume you have a CSV file containing historical prices of various financial assets. The dataset includes columns such as 'Date', 'Asset_1', 'Asset_2', ..., 'Asset_N'. Here's how to load and prepare the dataset:

```python
# Load the dataset
url = 'https://path-to-your-dataset.csv'
df = pd.read_csv(url, parse_dates=['Date'], index_col='Date')

# Display the first few rows of the dataset
print(df.head())
```

Calculating Correlation Matrix

The first step in visualizing correlations is to calculate the correlation matrix, which shows the pairwise correlation coefficients between the assets:

```python
# Calculate the correlation matrix
correlation_matrix = df.corr()

# Display the correlation matrix
print(correlation_matrix)
```

Visualizing the Correlation Matrix with Heatmaps

Heatmaps are an effective way to visualize correlation matrices. They use color gradients to represent correlation values, making it easy to identify strong positive or negative relationships at a glance.

1. Plotting the Heatmap:

```python
# Set up the matplotlib figure
plt.figure(figsize=(10, 8))

# Draw the heatmap with Seaborn
sns.heatmap(correlation_matrix,                annot=True,
cmap='coolwarm', vmin=-1, vmax=1)
```

```python
# Add titles and labels
plt.title('Correlation Matrix of Financial Assets')
plt.show()
```

Visualizing Pairwise Relationships with Pair Plots

Pair plots (or scatterplot matrices) allow you to visualize the relationships between pairs of assets, showing scatter plots for each pair and histograms for individual asset distributions.

1. Plotting the Pair Plot:

```python
# Select a subset of columns if the dataset is large
selected_assets = df[['Asset_1', 'Asset_2', 'Asset_3', 'Asset_4']]

# Plot the pair plot
sns.pairplot(selected_assets)

# Add a title
plt.suptitle('Pairwise Relationships Between Selected Assets', y=1.02)
plt.show()
```

Practical Applications

Portfolio Diversification

Understanding correlations between assets helps in constructing a diversified portfolio. Assets with low or negative correlations reduce portfolio risk, as losses in one asset may be offset by gains in another. Here's an example of how correlation analysis can inform portfolio choices:

- Diversification Strategy: If `Asset_A` and `Asset_B` have a correlation of -0.8, including both in a portfolio can reduce overall volatility.

Risk Management

Correlation analysis is vital for risk management. By identifying highly correlated assets, risk managers can anticipate systemic risks and implement hedging strategies to mitigate potential losses:

- Hedging Example: If `Asset_X` and `Asset_Y` are highly correlated, shorting `Asset_Y` can serve as a hedge against potential losses in `Asset_X`.

Advanced Visualization Techniques

Cluster Maps

Cluster maps extend heatmaps by grouping assets with similar correlation patterns, providing a hierarchical structure to the correlation matrix.

1. Plotting the Cluster Map:

```python
# Plot the cluster map
```

```
sns.clustermap(correlation_matrix,          annot=True,
cmap='coolwarm', vmin=-1, vmax=1)

# Add a title
plt.title('Cluster Map of Financial Asset Correlations')
plt.show()
```
` ` `

Dynamic Time-Warping (DTW)

Dynamic Time-Warping is an advanced technique used to measure similarity between time series that may vary in speed. It's particularly useful for comparing assets with differing volatility patterns.

1. Applying DTW (requires an additional library):

` ` `python
```
!pip install dtaidistance

from dtaidistance import dtw

# Compute the DTW distance between two assets
distance          =          dtw.distance(df['Asset_1'].values,
df['Asset_2'].values)

print(f'DTW Distance between Asset_1 and Asset_2:
{distance}')
```
` ` `

Combining Correlation Analysis with Moving Averages

Integrating correlation analysis with moving averages can provide a comprehensive view of market dynamics. Moving averages help smooth out price data, while correlation analysis reveals inter-asset relationships.

1. Plotting Moving Averages with Correlation Information:

```python
# Calculate moving averages
df['MA_Asset_1'] = df['Asset_1'].rolling(window=20).mean()
df['MA_Asset_2'] = df['Asset_2'].rolling(window=20).mean()

# Plot moving averages
plt.figure(figsize=(12, 6))
plt.plot(df.index, df['MA_Asset_1'], label='MA Asset 1')
plt.plot(df.index, df['MA_Asset_2'], label='MA Asset 2')

# Add correlation to the title
corr_value = df[['Asset_1', 'Asset_2']].corr().iloc[0, 1]
plt.title(f'Moving Averages with Correlation (Corr: {corr_value:.2f})')

plt.legend()
plt.show()
```

Visualizing correlations in financial data is a powerful technique for understanding market dynamics, enhancing portfolio management, and improving risk assessment. By leveraging Python libraries like Pandas and Seaborn, you can create insightful visualizations that reveal the intricate relationships between financial assets. Mastering these techniques will enable you to make more informed decisions, optimize your investment strategies, and conduct thorough financial analyses.

Incorporate these visualizations into your analytical toolkit to unlock deeper insights and foster a more nuanced understanding of financial markets. As you continue to explore and practice these methods, your proficiency in financial data analysis will grow, contributing to your success as a financial analyst.

Customizing Plot Aesthetics

Setting Up the Environment

To get started, ensure you have the necessary libraries installed. We'll primarily use Matplotlib for its versatility and Seaborn for its high-level interface and attractive default styles.

```python
!pip install matplotlib seaborn
```

Import the required libraries:

```python
```

```python
import matplotlib.pyplot as plt
import seaborn as sns
import pandas as pd
```

Basic Customization with Matplotlib

Matplotlib is highly customizable, allowing you to tweak almost every aspect of your plots. Here, we'll explore some foundational customization techniques.

1. Setting Plot Styles:

Matplotlib offers several built-in styles that can be easily applied to your plots. For example:

```python
plt.style.use('ggplot') # Apply ggplot style
```

2. Adjusting Plot Size:

You can specify the size of your plot using the `figsize` parameter:

```python
plt.figure(figsize=(12, 6)) # Set plot size
```

3. Adding Titles and Labels:

Titles and labels provide context to your plots:

```python
plt.title('Stock Prices Over Time')
plt.xlabel('Date')
plt.ylabel('Price')
```

4. Customizing Ticks and Gridlines:

Enhance readability by customizing ticks and gridlines:

```python
plt.xticks(rotation=45) # Rotate x-axis labels
plt.grid(True, linestyle='--', alpha=0.7) # Add gridlines
```

Advanced Customization with Seaborn

Seaborn builds on Matplotlib's capabilities, offering additional customization options and more attractive default styles.

1. Setting Seaborn Style:

Seaborn provides different styles such as 'darkgrid', 'whitegrid', 'dark', 'white', and 'ticks':

```python
sns.set_style('whitegrid') # Apply whitegrid style
```

``` ` ` ` ```

2. Color Palettes:

Seaborn has built-in color palettes that can be used to enhance your plots:

```python
sns.set_palette('husl') # Set color palette
```

3. Context Settings:

Adjust the context of your plots for different purposes such as 'paper', 'notebook', 'talk', and 'poster':

```python
sns.set_context('talk')    # Set context to 'talk' for
presentations
```

Creating Custom Legends

Legends help in identifying different elements in your plots. Customizing legends can improve the interpretability of your visualizations.

1. Adding Custom Legends:

```python
plt.plot(df['Date'], df['Asset_1'], label='Asset 1')
```
```

```python
plt.plot(df['Date'], df['Asset_2'], label='Asset 2')
plt.legend(title='Assets', loc='upper left')   # Add custom legend
```

2. Customizing Legend Appearance:

```python
legend = plt.legend(title='Assets')
plt.setp(legend.get_title(), fontsize='large')   # Customize legend title font size
plt.setp(legend.get_texts(), fontsize='medium') # Customize legend text font size
```

Enhancing Plot Aesthetics with Annotations

Annotations can be used to highlight specific data points or provide additional context.

1. Adding Text Annotations:

```python
plt.annotate('Significant Drop',
        xy=('2023-03-15', df.loc['2023-03-15', 'Asset_1']),
        xytext=('2023-02-15', df.loc['2023-03-15', 'Asset_1'] +5),
        arrowprops=dict(facecolor='red', shrink=0.05))
```

2. Adding Shape Annotations:

```python
plt.axvline(x='2023-03-15', color='grey', linestyle='--')   #
Vertical line

plt.axhspan(ymin=50, ymax=60, xmin=0.25, xmax=0.75,
color='yellow', alpha=0.3) # Highlight area
```

Customizing Plot Aesthetics for Financial Data

Financial data often requires specific customization techniques to make the plots more informative and visually appealing.

1. Candlestick and OHLC Charts:

Candlestick and OHLC charts are essential for visualizing price movements in financial markets. You can customize their aesthetics to enhance readability.

```python
import mplfinance as mpf

# Assuming `ohlc_data` is a DataFrame with columns
['Date', 'Open', 'High', 'Low', 'Close']
mpf.plot(ohlc_data,        type='candle',        style='charles',
title='Candlestick Chart', ylabel='Price')
```

2. Plotting Moving Averages:

Moving averages help in smoothing out price data to identify trends. Here's how to customize their appearance:

```python
df['MA_20'] = df['Asset_1'].rolling(window=20).mean()
df['MA_50'] = df['Asset_1'].rolling(window=50).mean()

plt.figure(figsize=(12, 6))
plt.plot(df['Date'], df['Asset_1'], label='Asset 1', color='blue')
plt.plot(df['Date'], df['MA_20'], label='20-Day MA', color='green', linestyle='--')
plt.plot(df['Date'], df['MA_50'], label='50-Day MA', color='red', linestyle='-.')
plt.title('Asset 1 with Moving Averages')
plt.xlabel('Date')
plt.ylabel('Price')
plt.legend()
plt.show()
```

3. Customizing Plot Aesthetics for Subplots:

When dealing with multiple subplots, ensure each subplot is well-labeled and aesthetically pleasing.

```python
fig, (ax1, ax2) = plt.subplots(2, 1, figsize=(12, 10),
```

```
sharex=True)

    # Plot on the first subplot
    ax1.plot(df['Date'], df['Asset_1'], label='Asset 1', color='blue')
    ax1.set_title('Asset 1 Prices')
    ax1.set_ylabel('Price')
    ax1.legend()

    # Plot on the second subplot
    ax2.plot(df['Date'], df['Asset_2'], label='Asset 2', color='green')
    ax2.set_title('Asset 2 Prices')
    ax2.set_xlabel('Date')
    ax2.set_ylabel('Price')
    ax2.legend()

    plt.tight_layout()
    plt.show()
    ` ` `
```

Practical Applications

Enhancing Reporting and Presentations

Customizing plot aesthetics is crucial for creating professional reports and presentations. By tailoring the appearance of your plots, you can ensure that your visualizations are clear, engaging, and effectively convey your analytical insights.

Improving Data Accessibility

Well-customized plots improve data accessibility for stakeholders who may not have a technical background. Clear labels, color-coding, and annotations help in making complex data more understandable.

Interactive Financial Dashboards with Plotly

Setting Up Your Environment

Before we dive into the creation process, ensure Plotly is installed in your environment. You can install it using pip:

```python
!pip install plotly
```

Import the necessary libraries:

```python
import plotly.graph_objs as go
import plotly.express as px
import pandas as pd
import json
```

Creating Your First Interactive Plot

Plotly simplifies the process of creating interactive plots. Let's start with a simple line chart to visualize stock prices over time.

1. Prepare Your DataFrame:

```python
# Sample data
data    =    {'Date':    pd.date_range(start='2023-01-01',
periods=100),
        'Stock_A': np.random.normal(100, 5, 100).cumsum(),
        'Stock_B': np.random.normal(120, 7, 100).cumsum()}

df = pd.DataFrame(data)
```

2. Create a Line Chart:

```python
fig = px.line(df, x='Date', y=['Stock_A', 'Stock_B'], title='Stock
Prices Over Time')
fig.show()
```

Building Interactive Financial Dashboards

Dashboards integrate various plots and controls, allowing users to interact with the data dynamically. Plotly Dash is an excellent tool for building web-based dashboards.

1. Install Dash:

```python
!pip install dash
```

2. Basic Layout of a Dash App:

```python
import dash
from dash import dcc, html
from dash.dependencies import Input, Output

app = dash.Dash(__name__)

app.layout = html.Div([
    html.H1("Interactive Financial Dashboard"),
    dcc.Dropdown(
        id='stock-dropdown',
        options=[
            {'label': 'Stock A', 'value': 'Stock_A'},
            {'label': 'Stock B', 'value': 'Stock_B'}
        ],
        value='Stock_A'
    ),
    dcc.Graph(id='price-chart')
])
```

3. Adding Interactivity:

To make the graph responsive to dropdown selections, we need to add a callback function.

```python
@app.callback(
    Output('price-chart', 'figure'),
    [Input('stock-dropdown', 'value')]
)
def update_chart(selected_stock):
    fig = px.line(df, x='Date', y=selected_stock, title=f'{selected_stock} Prices Over Time')
    return fig

if __name__ == '__main__':
    app.run_server(debug=True)
```

Advanced Customization in Dashboards

Interactive dashboards should be both visually appealing and functional. Here are several advanced customization techniques to enhance your dashboard's usability and aesthetics.

1. Adding Multiple Charts:

```python
```

```python
app.layout = html.Div([
    html.H1("Interactive Financial Dashboard"),
    dcc.Dropdown(
        id='stock-dropdown',
        options=[
            {'label': 'Stock A', 'value': 'Stock_A'},
            {'label': 'Stock B', 'value': 'Stock_B'}
        ],
        value='Stock_A'
    ),
    dcc.Graph(id='price-chart'),
    dcc.Graph(id='volume-chart')
])

@app.callback(
    [Output('price-chart', 'figure'),
     Output('volume-chart', 'figure')],
    [Input('stock-dropdown', 'value')]
)
def update_charts(selected_stock):
    price_fig = px.line(df, x='Date', y=selected_stock,
title=f'{selected_stock} Prices Over Time')
    volume_fig = px.bar(df, x='Date', y=selected_stock,
title=f'{selected_stock} Volume Over Time')
    return price_fig, volume_fig
```

2. Incorporating Financial Indicators:

Financial dashboards often benefit from additional indicators such as moving averages and Bollinger Bands.

```python
df['MA_20'] = df['Stock_A'].rolling(window=20).mean()
df['MA_50'] = df['Stock_A'].rolling(window=50).mean()

price_fig.add_trace(go.Scatter(x=df['Date'], y=df['MA_20'],
                    mode='lines', name='20-Day MA',
line=dict(dash='dash')))
price_fig.add_trace(go.Scatter(x=df['Date'], y=df['MA_50'],
                    mode='lines', name='50-Day MA',
line=dict(dash='dot')))
```

3. Enhancing Interactivity with Range Sliders:

Range sliders allow users to zoom into specific time periods easily.

```python
price_fig.update_layout(
    xaxis=dict(
        rangeselector=dict(
        buttons=list([
            dict(count=1, label="1m", step="month",
stepmode="backward"),
            dict(count=6, label="6m", step="month",
stepmode="backward"),
```

```
            dict(step="all")
        ])
    ),
    rangeslider=dict(visible=True),
    type="date"
  )
)
```
` ` `

Practical Applications

Real-Time Data Integration

Integrating APIs for real-time data feeds can make your dashboards incredibly powerful. For instance, you can connect to financial data APIs like Alpha Vantage or Yahoo Finance to fetch live market data.

1. Fetching Real-Time Data:

```python
import yfinance as yf

def fetch_data(ticker):
    return yf.download(ticker, period='1d', interval='1m')

df_live = fetch_data('AAPL')
```
` ` `

2. Updating Dashboards with Real-Time Data:

```python
@app.callback(
    Output('live-price-chart', 'figure'),
    Input('interval-component', 'n_intervals')
)
def update_live_data(n):
    df_live = fetch_data('AAPL')
    fig = px.line(df_live, x=df_live.index, y='Close', title='Live AAPL Prices')
    return fig

app.layout = html.Div([
    dcc.Interval(id='interval-component', interval=60*1000, n_intervals=0), # Update every minute
    dcc.Graph(id='live-price-chart')
])
```

Customizing User Experience

A well-designed user interface (UI) enhances the user's ability to interact effectively with the dashboard. Consider the following tips for improving user experience:

1. Responsive Layouts:

Dash allows for responsive layouts that adjust to different screen sizes. Use the `style` attribute and `className` to create flexible designs.

```python
app.layout = html.Div([
    html.Div([
        dcc.Dropdown(id='stock-dropdown',        options=[...],
value='Stock_A')
    ], className='six columns'),
    html.Div([
        dcc.Graph(id='price-chart')
    ], className='six columns')
], className='row')
```

2. Loading States:

Indicate loading states to users when data is being fetched or updated.

```python
app.layout = html.Div([
    dcc.Loading(
        id="loading-1",
        type="default",
        children=html.Div([dcc.Graph(id='price-chart')])
    )
])
```

Interactive financial dashboards with Plotly provide an

unparalleled level of engagement, allowing analysts and stakeholders to dive deep into data and uncover hidden insights. By leveraging the power of Plotly and Dash, you can build dynamic, real-time visualizations that not only enhance data comprehension but also facilitate informed decision-making. Incorporate these techniques into your workflow to transform raw financial data into interactive, insightful dashboards that drive clarity and action.

Case Studies: Visualizing Real-World Financial Data

Case Study 1: Analyzing Stock Market Trends

Objective: To analyze the performance of multiple stocks over time and identify trends and patterns.

Data Source: Historical stock prices for a selection of tech companies (e.g., Apple, Microsoft, Google) obtained from a public API such as Yahoo Finance.

1. Fetching the Data:

```python
import yfinance as yf

tickers = ['AAPL', 'MSFT', 'GOOGL']
stock_data = yf.download(tickers, start='2020-01-01', end='2023-01-01')
```

2. Preparing the Data:

```python
stock_data = stock_data['Adj Close']
stock_data.reset_index(inplace=True)
```

3. Creating Interactive Line Charts:

```python
import plotly.express as px

fig = px.line(stock_data, x='Date', y=stock_data.columns[1:], title='Stock Prices Over Time')
fig.update_layout(xaxis_title='Date', yaxis_title='Adjusted Closing Price')
fig.show()
```

Insights: By visualizing stock prices over time, we can easily identify trends, such as periods of rapid growth or downturns. This allows investors to make more informed decisions based on historical performance.

Case Study 2: Portfolio Performance Analysis

Objective: To evaluate the performance of a financial portfolio comprising different assets and analyze the contributions of each asset to the overall return.

Data Source: Historical data for a mix of stocks, bonds, and ETFs.

1. Fetching and Preparing the Data:

```python
portfolio_tickers = ['AAPL', 'MSFT', 'TLT', 'SPY']
portfolio_data = yf.download(portfolio_tickers, start='2020-01-01', end='2023-01-01')
portfolio_data = portfolio_data['Adj Close']
portfolio_data.reset_index(inplace=True)
```

2. Calculating Portfolio Returns:

```python
portfolio_data['Portfolio'] = portfolio_data.mean(axis=1)
portfolio_data['Returns'] = portfolio_data['Portfolio'].pct_change()
```

3. Creating Cumulative Returns Chart:

```python
portfolio_data['Cumulative Returns'] = (1 + portfolio_data['Returns']).cumprod()

fig = px.line(portfolio_data, x='Date', y='Cumulative Returns', title='Portfolio Cumulative Returns Over Time')
```

```
fig.update_layout(xaxis_title='Date',
yaxis_title='Cumulative Returns')
    fig.show()
    ` ` `
```

Insights: This visualization helps in understanding how the portfolio has grown over time and the impact of different assets. It can also aid in identifying periods of high volatility and stability.

Case Study 3: Visualizing Correlations in Financial Data

Objective: To explore the relationships between various financial instruments and visualize their correlations.

Data Source: Historical data for a diverse set of assets, including stocks, bonds, and commodities.

1. Fetching and Preparing the Data:

```python
assets_tickers = ['AAPL', 'MSFT', 'GLD', 'TLT', 'SPY']
assets_data        =        yf.download(assets_tickers,
start='2020-01-01', end='2023-01-01')
    assets_data = assets_data['Adj Close']
    ` ` `
```

2. Calculating Correlation Matrix:

```python
correlation_matrix = assets_data.corr()
```

` ` `

3. Creating a Heatmap:

```python
import plotly.figure_factory as ff

fig = ff.create_annotated_heatmap(
    z=correlation_matrix.values,
    x=list(correlation_matrix.columns),
    y=list(correlation_matrix.index),
    colorscale='Viridis',
    annotation_text=correlation_matrix.round(2).values
)
fig.update_layout(title='Correlation Matrix of Financial Instruments')
fig.show()
```

Insights: The heatmap reveals the strength and direction of relationships between different assets. High positive correlations suggest that assets move together, while negative correlations indicate inverse relationships. This information is vital for diversification strategies.

Case Study 4: Real-Time Trading Dashboard

Objective: To create a real-time trading dashboard that updates live stock prices and provides insights into market movements.

Data Source: Live data from a financial API such as Alpha Vantage or Yahoo Finance.

1. Fetching Real-Time Data:

```python
import yfinance as yf

def fetch_live_data(ticker):
    return yf.download(ticker, period='1d', interval='1m')

live_data = fetch_live_data('AAPL')
```

2. Creating a Real-Time Line Chart:

```python
app = dash.Dash(__name__)

app.layout = html.Div([
    dcc.Interval(id='interval-component', interval=60*1000, n_intervals=0),
    dcc.Graph(id='live-price-chart')
])

@app.callback(
    Output('live-price-chart', 'figure'),
    Input('interval-component', 'n_intervals')
)
```

```python
def update_live_chart(n):
    live_data = fetch_live_data('AAPL')
    fig = px.line(live_data, x=live_data.index, y='Close',
title='Live AAPL Prices')
    return fig

if __name__ == '__main__':
    app.run_server(debug=True)
```

Insights: A real-time trading dashboard is a powerful tool for traders, providing up-to-the-minute data that can inform buying and selling decisions. By visualizing live price movements, traders can react swiftly to market changes.

Case Study 5: Economic Indicator Analysis

Objective: To analyze and visualize key economic indicators and their impact on the financial markets.

Data Source: Publicly available economic data from sources such as the Federal Reserve Economic Data (FRED) or World Bank.

1. Fetching Economic Data:

```python
import pandas_datareader as web

gdp = web.DataReader('GDP', 'fred', start='2000-01-01',
end='2023-01-01')
```

```python
inflation = web.DataReader('CPIAUCSL', 'fred',
start='2000-01-01', end='2023-01-01')
```

2. Combining and Preparing Data:

```python
economic_data = pd.concat([gdp, inflation], axis=1)
economic_data.columns = ['GDP', 'Inflation']
economic_data.reset_index(inplace=True)
```

3. Creating Multi-Axis Line Chart:

```python
fig = make_subplots(specs=[[{"secondary_y": True}]])

fig.add_trace(
    go.Scatter(x=economic_data['DATE'],
y=economic_data['GDP'], name='GDP'),
    secondary_y=False,
)

fig.add_trace(
    go.Scatter(x=economic_data['DATE'],
y=economic_data['Inflation'], name='Inflation'),
    secondary_y=True,
)
```

```
fig.update_layout(
    title='GDP and Inflation Over Time',
    xaxis_title='Date',
    yaxis_title='GDP',
    yaxis2_title='Inflation'
)

fig.show()
```
```

Insights: Visualizing economic indicators against market performance helps in understanding macroeconomic impacts. Analysts can correlate economic conditions with market trends, aiding in strategic planning and forecasting.

These case studies showcase the practical application of Pandas and Plotly in visualizing real-world financial data. By leveraging these powerful libraries, analysts can transform raw data into insightful visualizations that drive informed decision-making. Whether analyzing stock trends, evaluating portfolio performance, exploring asset correlations, building real-time dashboards, or assessing economic indicators, the techniques demonstrated here provide a robust foundation for advanced financial analysis.
```

CHAPTER 4: PORTFOLIO ANALYSIS AND OPTIMIZATION

Portfolio theory, a cornerstone of modern finance, provides a framework for constructing an investment portfolio that aims to optimize returns while managing risk. Developed by Harry Markowitz in the 1950s, this theory revolutionized the way financial analysts and investors approach asset allocation. At its core, portfolio theory emphasizes the importance of diversification and the interplay between risk and return, offering a systematic method to balance the trade-offs inherent in investment decisions.

The Concept of Risk and Return

At the heart of portfolio theory lies the fundamental relationship between risk and return. Investors are constantly seeking the highest possible returns, but these returns come with varying levels of risk. In financial terms, risk is often quantified as the standard deviation of returns, which measures the volatility or variability of an asset's performance. Return, on the other hand, is typically the mean or expected value of these returns.

To illustrate, let's consider two financial assets: a government bond and a tech stock. The government bond, known for its stability, offers lower returns but with minimal risk. Conversely, the tech stock, while potentially offering higher returns, comes with significant volatility. Portfolio theory suggests that by combining these two assets, an investor can achieve a more desirable balance of risk and return.

Diversification: The Free Lunch

Markowitz's groundbreaking insight was that diversification —spreading investments across a variety of assets—could reduce risk without necessarily sacrificing returns. The old adage, "Don't put all your eggs in one basket," perfectly encapsulates this principle. By holding a diversified portfolio, the poor performance of one asset can be offset by the strong performance of another, thus smoothing out overall portfolio returns.

Consider an example with Python:

```python
import pandas as pd
import numpy as np

# Simulate returns for two assets
np.random.seed(42)
returns_asset_1 = np.random.normal(0.10, 0.15, 1000) #
```

Expected return 10%, volatility 15%

returns_asset_2 = np.random.normal(0.15, 0.25, 1000) # Expected return 15%, volatility 25%

```
# Create a DataFrame
returns = pd.DataFrame({'Asset_1': returns_asset_1, 'Asset_2': returns_asset_2})

# Calculate the portfolio return and risk
portfolio_weights = np.array([0.5, 0.5])
portfolio_returns = returns.dot(portfolio_weights)
portfolio_risk = np.std(portfolio_returns)

print(f"Portfolio Return: {portfolio_returns.mean():.2f}")
print(f"Portfolio Risk: {portfolio_risk:.2f}")
```
` ` `

This code snippet demonstrates how portfolio theory can be applied using the Pandas library. By simulating returns for two assets and calculating the portfolio's overall return and risk, we can visualize the benefits of diversification.

The Efficient Frontier

Markowitz also introduced the concept of the efficient frontier, a graphical representation of the optimal portfolios offering the highest expected return for a given level of risk. Portfolios that lie on the efficient frontier are considered optimal, as no other portfolio can provide a better return-to-risk ratio.

To plot the efficient frontier, one can run a series of

simulations to generate various portfolio combinations and then calculate their respective risks and returns. Here's a practical demonstration:

```python
import matplotlib.pyplot as plt

# Function to calculate portfolio performance
def portfolio_performance(weights, returns):
    port_return = np.dot(weights, returns.mean())
    port_risk = np.sqrt(np.dot(weights.T, np.dot(returns.cov(), weights)))
    return port_return, port_risk

# Generate random portfolios
num_portfolios = 10000
results = np.zeros((3, num_portfolios))
for i in range(num_portfolios):
    weights = np.random.random(2)
    weights /= np.sum(weights)
    port_return, port_risk = portfolio_performance(weights, returns)
    results[0,i] = port_return
    results[1,i] = port_risk
    results[2,i] = port_return / port_risk

# Plot the efficient frontier
plt.figure(figsize=(10, 6))
plt.scatter(results[1,:],        results[0,:],        c=results[2,:],
```

```
cmap='viridis', marker='o')
plt.xlabel('Risk (Standard Deviation)')
plt.ylabel('Return')
plt.colorbar(label='Sharpe Ratio')
plt.title('Efficient Frontier')
plt.show()
```

This script generates random portfolios and plots the efficient frontier, showcasing the trade-offs between risk and return. The colour gradient represents the Sharpe Ratio, a measure of risk-adjusted return, further aiding in identifying optimal portfolios.

The Capital Market Line and the Sharpe Ratio

The Capital Market Line (CML) and the Sharpe Ratio are pivotal concepts derived from the Capital Asset Pricing Model (CAPM). The CML represents portfolios that optimally combine a risk-free asset with the market portfolio, providing a benchmark for evaluating portfolio performance. The Sharpe Ratio, calculated as the excess return per unit of risk, allows investors to compare the risk-adjusted performance of different portfolios.

For a practical implementation:

```python
# Assume risk-free rate is 2%
risk_free_rate = 0.02
```

```
# Calculate Sharpe Ratios
sharpe_ratios = (results[0,:] - risk_free_rate) / results[1,:]

# Plot the Capital Market Line
plt.figure(figsize=(10, 6))
plt.scatter(results[1,:], results[0,:], c=sharpe_ratios, cmap='viridis', marker='o')
plt.plot([0, max(results[1,:])], [risk_free_rate, risk_free_rate + max(sharpe_ratios) * max(results[1,:])], color='red', label='CML')
plt.xlabel('Risk (Standard Deviation)')
plt.ylabel('Return')
plt.colorbar(label='Sharpe Ratio')
plt.legend()
plt.title('Capital Market Line and Efficient Frontier')
plt.show()
```
```

Plotting the CML, investors can visually assess whether their portfolios are achieving superior risk-adjusted returns relative to the market.

The introduction to portfolio theory lays the foundational understanding required for advancing into more complex areas of financial analysis and portfolio optimization. By grasping the principles of diversification, the efficient frontier, and risk-return dynamics, you are better equipped to construct robust portfolios that align with your investment objectives.
```

Creating and Managing a Financial Portfolio with Pandas

Setting Up Your Environment

Before diving into portfolio creation, ensure that you have Pandas installed. You can set up your environment by running:

```bash
pip install pandas
```

Additionally, install other essential libraries like NumPy and Matplotlib for numerical operations and data visualization:

```bash
pip install numpy matplotlib
```

Importing and Preparing Data

Start by importing necessary libraries and loading financial data. For this example, let's assume you have historical stock prices for a selection of assets.

```python
import pandas as pd
import numpy as np
import matplotlib.pyplot as plt
```

```
# Read historical stock price data
tickers = ['AAPL', 'MSFT', 'GOOG', 'AMZN']
data = pd.DataFrame()

for ticker in tickers:
    data[ticker]        =        pd.read_csv(f'data/{ticker}.csv',
index_col='Date', parse_dates=True)['Adj Close']
```

This script reads adjusted closing prices for Apple, Microsoft, Google, and Amazon from CSV files and stores them in a Pandas DataFrame. Ensure that the CSV files are properly formatted and contain historical price data.

Calculating Daily Returns

Next, calculate the daily returns for each asset. Daily returns are essential for understanding portfolio performance and risk.

```python
returns = data.pct_change().dropna()
```

The `pct_change()` function computes the percentage change between the current and prior elements, effectively giving you the daily returns. The `dropna()` method removes any rows with missing values that may result from this calculation.

Constructing the Portfolio

To construct a portfolio, assign weights to each asset. Weights represent the proportion of the total investment allocated to each asset. Sum of all weights should equal 1.

```python
# Example weights: 25% each
weights = np.array([0.25, 0.25, 0.25, 0.25])
```

Calculating Portfolio Returns and Risk

With the daily returns and weights, you can calculate the portfolio's returns and risk.

```python
# Calculate portfolio returns
portfolio_returns = returns.dot(weights)

# Calculate portfolio risk (standard deviation)
portfolio_risk = np.std(portfolio_returns)

print(f"Portfolio Return: {portfolio_returns.mean():.2%}")
print(f"Portfolio Risk: {portfolio_risk:.2%}")
```

Here, the `dot()` method multiplies the returns by the weights and sums them up, giving the portfolio's daily returns. The standard deviation of these returns represents the portfolio's risk.

Portfolio Performance Visualization

Visualizing the performance of your portfolio helps in tracking trends and making data-driven decisions.

```python
plt.figure(figsize=(10,6))
plt.plot(data.index, (1 + portfolio_returns).cumprod(), label='Portfolio')
for ticker in tickers:
    plt.plot(data.index, (1 + returns[ticker]).cumprod(), label=ticker)
plt.xlabel('Date')
plt.ylabel('Cumulative Returns')
plt.legend()
plt.title('Portfolio Performance vs Individual Stocks')
plt.show()
```

This plot displays the cumulative returns of the portfolio compared to individual assets, providing a visual benchmark for portfolio performance.

Rebalancing the Portfolio

Over time, the asset weights in your portfolio may drift due to differential performance. Rebalancing involves adjusting the portfolio back to its target weights.

```python
def rebalance_portfolio(data, target_weights, rebalance_dates):
    current_weights = target_weights.copy()
    portfolio_value = 1
    portfolio_values = []

    for date in data.index:
        if date in rebalance_dates:
            portfolio_value = (portfolio_value * (1 + returns.loc[date].dot(current_weights)))
            current_weights = target_weights.copy()
        else:
            portfolio_value *= (1 + returns.loc[date].dot(current_weights))
        portfolio_values.append(portfolio_value)

    return pd.Series(portfolio_values, index=data.index)

# Example rebalancing every quarter
rebalance_dates = pd.date_range(start='2015-01-01', end='2020-01-01', freq='Q')
balanced_portfolio = rebalance_portfolio(data, weights, rebalance_dates)

plt.figure(figsize=(10,6))
plt.plot(balanced_portfolio, label='Rebalanced Portfolio')
plt.xlabel('Date')
```

```python
plt.ylabel('Cumulative Returns')
plt.legend()
plt.title('Rebalanced Portfolio Performance')
plt.show()
```

This function rebalance the portfolio at specified dates, maintaining the target allocation. The resulting series represents the cumulative returns of the rebalanced portfolio.

Adjusting Portfolio Allocation

Based on market conditions or changes in investment objectives, you might need to adjust your portfolio allocation. Pandas allows you to simulate different scenarios and assess their impact.

```python
# New weights example: higher allocation to technology stocks
new_weights = np.array([0.10, 0.10, 0.40, 0.40])
new_portfolio_returns = returns.dot(new_weights)

plt.figure(figsize=(10,6))
plt.plot(data.index, (1 + new_portfolio_returns).cumprod(), label='Adjusted Portfolio')
plt.xlabel('Date')
plt.ylabel('Cumulative Returns')
plt.legend()
plt.title('Adjusted Portfolio Performance')
```

```
plt.show()

new_portfolio_risk = np.std(new_portfolio_returns)
print(f"Adjusted                Portfolio                Return:
{new_portfolio_returns.mean():.2%}")
print(f"Adjusted Portfolio Risk: {new_portfolio_risk:.2%}")
` ` `
```

This adjustment demonstrates how changing asset weights can affect portfolio performance and risk.

Creating and managing a financial portfolio with Pandas empowers you to harness the full potential of your investment strategy. By calculating returns, visualizing performance, rebalancing, and adjusting allocations, you can make informed decisions that align with your financial goals. As you continue to delve deeper into portfolio analysis and optimization, remember that Pandas provides a robust framework for handling these tasks with precision and efficiency.

Calculating Portfolio Returns and Risk

Setting Up Your Environment

Before delving into calculations, ensure that you have Pandas installed along with essential libraries like NumPy for numerical operations and Matplotlib for visualization:

```bash
pip install pandas numpy matplotlib
```

```
` ` `
```

Importing and Preparing Data

Begin by importing the necessary libraries and loading your financial data. For this example, let's assume you have historical stock prices for a selection of assets.

```python
import pandas as pd
import numpy as np
import matplotlib.pyplot as plt

# Read historical stock price data
tickers = ['AAPL', 'MSFT', 'GOOG', 'AMZN']
data = pd.DataFrame()

for ticker in tickers:
    data[ticker] = pd.read_csv(f'data/{ticker}.csv', index_col='Date', parse_dates=True)['Adj Close']
```

This script reads adjusted closing prices for Apple, Microsoft, Google, and Amazon from CSV files and stores them in a Pandas DataFrame. Ensure that the CSV files are properly formatted and contain historical price data.

Calculating Daily Returns

Daily returns are fundamental to understanding portfolio performance. Calculate the daily returns for each asset as follows:

```python
returns = data.pct_change().dropna()
```

The `pct_change()` function computes the percentage change between the current and prior elements, effectively giving you the daily returns. The `dropna()` method removes any rows with missing values that may result from this calculation.

Assigning Weights to Portfolio Assets

To construct a portfolio, assign weights to each asset. The weights represent the proportion of the total investment allocated to each asset. Ensure that the sum of all weights equals 1.

```python
# Example weights: 25% each
weights = np.array([0.25, 0.25, 0.25, 0.25])
```

Calculating Portfolio Returns

With the daily returns and weights defined, you can calculate the portfolio's returns. This involves taking the dot product of the returns DataFrame and the weights array.

```python
# Calculate portfolio returns
```

```
portfolio_returns = returns.dot(weights)

# Display the first few rows of portfolio returns
print(portfolio_returns.head())
```

The `dot()` method multiplies the returns by the weights and sums them up, giving the portfolio's daily returns.

Calculating Portfolio Risk

Portfolio risk is typically measured using the standard deviation of the portfolio returns. This metric indicates the volatility or variability of returns.

```python
# Calculate portfolio risk (standard deviation)
portfolio_risk = np.std(portfolio_returns)

print(f"Portfolio Risk: {portfolio_risk:.2%}")
```

The standard deviation provides a sense of how much the portfolio returns fluctuate over time.

Visualizing Portfolio Performance

Visualizing the performance of your portfolio helps in tracking trends and making data-driven decisions.

```python
```

```python
plt.figure(figsize=(10,6))
plt.plot(data.index, (1 + portfolio_returns).cumprod(), label='Portfolio')
for ticker in tickers:
    plt.plot(data.index, (1 + returns[ticker]).cumprod(), label=ticker)
plt.xlabel('Date')
plt.ylabel('Cumulative Returns')
plt.legend()
plt.title('Portfolio Performance vs Individual Stocks')
plt.show()
```

This plot displays the cumulative returns of the portfolio compared to individual assets, providing a visual benchmark for portfolio performance.

Advanced Portfolio Metrics

Beyond simple returns and risk, more sophisticated metrics like the Sharpe Ratio can provide deeper insights into portfolio performance. The Sharpe Ratio measures the risk-adjusted return of the portfolio.

```python
# Assumed risk-free rate (e.g., 1.5% annualized)
risk_free_rate = 0.015 / 252 # daily risk-free rate

# Calculate excess returns
excess_returns = portfolio_returns - risk_free_rate
```

```python
# Calculate Sharpe Ratio
sharpe_ratio = np.mean(excess_returns) / np.std(excess_returns) * np.sqrt(252)

print(f"Sharpe Ratio: {sharpe_ratio:.2f}")
```

The Sharpe Ratio is computed by dividing the mean of the excess returns by the standard deviation of the excess returns and then annualizing the result by multiplying by the square root of the number of trading days (typically 252).

Stress Testing the Portfolio

Stress testing involves simulating adverse market conditions to evaluate portfolio resilience. Pandas allows you to model different stress scenarios and observe their impact.

```python
# Hypothetical market downturn scenario (e.g., 10% drop in all asset prices)
stress_returns = returns - 0.10

# Calculate stressed portfolio returns
stressed_portfolio_returns = stress_returns.dot(weights)

# Calculate cumulative returns under stress
cumulative_stressed_returns = (1 + stressed_portfolio_returns).cumprod()
```

```python
plt.figure(figsize=(10,6))
plt.plot(data.index,            cumulative_stressed_returns,
label='Stressed Portfolio')
plt.xlabel('Date')
plt.ylabel('Cumulative Returns')
plt.legend()
plt.title('Portfolio Performance Under Stress Scenario')
plt.show()
```

This stress test models a hypothetical market downturn, adjusting the returns accordingly and visualizing the portfolio's performance under these conditions.

Scenario Analysis and Adjusting Portfolio Allocation

Market conditions and investment objectives may change over time, necessitating adjustments to your portfolio allocation. Pandas enables you to simulate different scenarios and assess their impact.

```python
# New weights example: higher allocation to technology stocks
new_weights = np.array([0.10, 0.10, 0.40, 0.40])
new_portfolio_returns = returns.dot(new_weights)

plt.figure(figsize=(10,6))
plt.plot(data.index, (1 + new_portfolio_returns).cumprod(),
```

```
label='Adjusted Portfolio')
plt.xlabel('Date')
plt.ylabel('Cumulative Returns')
plt.legend()
plt.title('Adjusted Portfolio Performance')
plt.show()

new_portfolio_risk = np.std(new_portfolio_returns)
print(f"Adjusted                Portfolio               Return:
{new_portfolio_returns.mean():.2%}")
print(f"Adjusted Portfolio Risk: {new_portfolio_risk:.2%}")
```
```

This adjustment demonstrates how changing asset weights can affect portfolio performance and risk, allowing you to optimize based on new information or strategic shifts.

Calculating portfolio returns and risk with Pandas equips you with the tools to analyze and optimize your investments rigorously. By understanding and applying these metrics, you can make informed decisions that align with your financial goals, ensuring that your portfolio remains resilient and poised for growth in varying market conditions.

Diversification and Covariance Matrix

# Understanding Diversification
```

Diversification involves creating a portfolio consisting of various assets to smooth out the impact of any single asset's volatility. By diversifying, you are not putting all your eggs in one basket, which helps to reduce the overall risk. The goal is to combine assets that do not perfectly correlate, thus ensuring that the portfolio's performance is not overly dependent on any one investment.

Let's begin by setting up the environment and loading some sample data.

```bash
pip install pandas numpy matplotlib
```

Importing and Preparing Data

First, import the necessary libraries and load historical stock price data for a set of assets. This example uses daily adjusted closing prices for a selection of stocks.

```python
import pandas as pd
import numpy as np
import matplotlib.pyplot as plt

# Read historical stock price data
tickers = ['AAPL', 'MSFT', 'GOOG', 'AMZN']
data = pd.DataFrame()
```

for ticker in tickers:

```
    data[ticker]         =          pd.read_csv(f'data/{ticker}.csv',
index_col='Date', parse_dates=True)['Adj Close']
```

Ensure that the CSV files contain historical prices with the correct formatting.

Calculating Daily Returns

Calculate the daily returns for each asset to analyze how they have historically performed.

```python
returns = data.pct_change().dropna()
```

The `pct_change()` function computes the daily percentage change, and `dropna()` eliminates any rows with missing values.

Constructing the Covariance Matrix

The covariance matrix provides a measure of how returns on two assets move together. Positive covariance indicates that asset returns move in the same direction, while negative covariance indicates the opposite.

```python
cov_matrix = returns.cov()
```

```
print(cov_matrix)
```
```

```

The `cov()` method calculates the covariance matrix of the daily returns DataFrame. Each element in this matrix represents the covariance between two assets.

Interpreting the Covariance Matrix

Each element in the covariance matrix gives insights into the relationship between pairs of assets. For instance, a high positive value between two assets suggests they tend to increase or decrease simultaneously. Conversely, a high negative value indicates that when one asset's return increases, the other's decreases.

To visualize the covariance matrix:

```python
plt.imshow(cov_matrix,                      cmap='coolwarm',
interpolation='none')
plt.colorbar()
plt.xticks(range(len(cov_matrix)),          cov_matrix.columns,
rotation=90)
plt.yticks(range(len(cov_matrix)), cov_matrix.columns)
plt.title('Covariance Matrix')
plt.show()
```
```

```

This heatmap provides a visual representation of the covariance values, making it easier to identify relationships between assets.

Diversification Strategy

To construct a diversified portfolio, ideally, you want to combine assets with low or negative covariance. By doing so, the overall portfolio risk can be reduced without necessarily sacrificing returns.

Suppose you have the following weights for your assets:

```python
weights = np.array([0.25, 0.25, 0.25, 0.25])
```

Calculating Portfolio Variance and Standard Deviation

Using the covariance matrix and the weights, you can compute the portfolio variance and standard deviation, which are essential measures of risk.

```python
# Portfolio variance
portfolio_variance = np.dot(weights.T, np.dot(cov_matrix, weights))
print(f"Portfolio Variance: {portfolio_variance:.6f}")

# Portfolio standard deviation (risk)
portfolio_std_dev = np.sqrt(portfolio_variance)
print(f"Portfolio Standard Deviation: {portfolio_std_dev:.2%}")
```

```
` ` `
```

The variance is calculated using the formula $\(\sigma\_p^2 = w^T \Sigma w\)$, where $\(w\)$ is the weight vector and $\(\Sigma\)$ is the covariance matrix. The standard deviation is simply the square root of the variance, providing a tangible measure of risk.

Visualizing Diversification Impact

To visualize how diversification impacts portfolio risk, compare the portfolio's standard deviation to the individual standard deviations of the assets.

```python
# Individual asset standard deviations
individual_std_devs = returns.std()
print(individual_std_devs)

# Plot
plt.figure(figsize=(10,6))
plt.bar(tickers, individual_std_devs, label='Individual Asset Risk')
plt.bar(['Portfolio'], portfolio_std_dev, label='Portfolio Risk', color='red')
plt.ylabel('Standard Deviation (Risk)')
plt.legend()
plt.title('Risk Comparison: Individual Assets vs. Portfolio')
plt.show()
` ` `
```

This bar chart illustrates the risk reduction achieved through diversification, demonstrating that the portfolio's standard deviation is lower than the average of the individual assets' standard deviations.

Real-World Application: Constructing a Diversified Portfolio

Consider a real-world example where you want to construct a diversified portfolio using not just stocks, but also bonds and other asset classes. Integrating multiple asset classes can further enhance diversification.

```python
# Suppose you have additional data for bonds and commodities
# Example: 'BONDS', 'COMMODITIES'
additional_tickers = ['BONDS', 'COMMODITIES']
for ticker in additional_tickers:
    data[ticker]        =        pd.read_csv(f'data/{ticker}.csv', index_col='Date', parse_dates=True)['Adj Close']

# Recalculate daily returns including the new assets
returns = data.pct_change().dropna()

# Update covariance matrix
cov_matrix = returns.cov()

# New weights example: diversified across more asset classes
weights = np.array([0.20, 0.20, 0.20, 0.20, 0.10, 0.10])
```

```
# Recalculate portfolio variance and standard deviation
portfolio_variance = np.dot(weights.T, np.dot(cov_matrix, weights))
portfolio_std_dev = np.sqrt(portfolio_variance)

print(f"Updated Portfolio Standard Deviation: {portfolio_std_dev:.2%}")
```

This expanded diversification approach includes bonds and commodities, further reducing risk by incorporating different asset classes that may not correlate strongly with equities.

Understanding diversification and the covariance matrix is essential for constructing a robust, low-risk portfolio. Utilizing Pandas, you can effectively compute and visualize these metrics, enabling you to create well-diversified portfolios that align with your financial goals. By leveraging the principles of diversification and quantitative analysis, you can enhance your investment strategy, minimize risk, and optimize returns.

This detailed exploration of diversification and the covariance matrix equips you with the knowledge to make informed, data-driven investment decisions, ensuring a resilient and well-balanced portfolio.

Mean-Variance Optimization

Understanding Mean-Variance Optimization

At its core, mean-variance optimization involves the following steps:

1. Estimating Expected Returns: Predicting the future returns of assets based on historical data.

2. Calculating Covariance Matrix: Assessing the degree to which the returns of different assets move together.

3. Optimization: Identifying the asset weights that either minimize risk for a given return or maximize return for a given risk.

Setting Up the Environment

First, ensure that you have the necessary libraries installed and import them into your Python environment.

```bash
pip install pandas numpy matplotlib scipy
```

```python
import pandas as pd
import numpy as np
import matplotlib.pyplot as plt
from scipy.optimize import minimize
```

Importing and Preparing Data

Load historical stock price data for a set of assets. This example uses daily adjusted closing prices for a selection of stocks.

```python
tickers = ['AAPL', 'MSFT', 'GOOG', 'AMZN']
data = pd.DataFrame()

for ticker in tickers:
    data[ticker] = pd.read_csv(f'data/{ticker}.csv', index_col='Date', parse_dates=True)['Adj Close']
```

Ensure that the CSV files contain historical prices with the correct formatting.

Calculating Daily Returns and Expected Returns

Compute the daily returns and then calculate the expected annual returns for each asset.

```python
# Calculate daily returns
returns = data.pct_change().dropna()

# Calculate expected annual returns
expected_returns = returns.mean() * 252
```

Here, we multiply the mean daily return by 252 to annualize it, assuming there are 252 trading days in a year.

Constructing the Covariance Matrix

Calculate the covariance matrix of the daily returns, which will be used to assess the risk (volatility) of the portfolio.

```python
cov_matrix = returns.cov() * 252  # Annualize the covariance
matrix
```

Defining the Optimization Problem

To optimize the portfolio, we aim to minimize the portfolio variance subject to certain constraints. The key constraints include:

1. The sum of the asset weights must be 1 (i.e., the entire capital is invested).

2. The asset weights must be non-negative (i.e., no short selling).

Define the functions for calculating the portfolio return and portfolio variance.

```python
def portfolio_return(weights, expected_returns):
    return np.dot(weights, expected_returns)

def portfolio_variance(weights, cov_matrix):
```

```
    return np.dot(weights.T, np.dot(cov_matrix, weights))
```
` ` `

Optimization Process

Use the `minimize` function from the `scipy.optimize` package to find the optimal weights.

` ` `python
```python
def optimize_portfolio(expected_returns, cov_matrix):
    num_assets = len(expected_returns)
    args = (expected_returns, cov_matrix)

    # Constraints: Sum of weights is 1
    constraints = ({'type': 'eq', 'fun': lambda x: np.sum(x) - 1})

    # Bounds: No short selling (weights between 0 and 1)
    bounds = tuple((0, 1) for _ in range(num_assets))

    # Initial guess: Equal distribution
    init_guess = num_assets * [1. / num_assets]

    # Minimize portfolio variance
    result = minimize(portfolio_variance, init_guess, args=args, method='SLSQP', bounds=bounds, constraints=constraints)

    return result.x

optimal_weights = optimize_portfolio(expected_returns,
```

```python
cov_matrix)
print(f"Optimal Weights: {optimal_weights}")
```

Visualizing the Efficient Frontier

The efficient frontier represents the set of optimal portfolios that offer the highest expected return for a given level of risk. To plot the efficient frontier, calculate the risk and return for a range of portfolios with different asset weights.

```python
def    efficient_frontier(expected_returns,    cov_matrix,
num_portfolios=100):
    results = np.zeros((3, num_portfolios))
    weights_record = []

    for i in range(num_portfolios):
        weights = np.random.random(len(expected_returns))
        weights /= np.sum(weights)
        weights_record.append(weights)
        portfolio_return_value   =   portfolio_return(weights,
expected_returns)
        portfolio_variance_value = portfolio_variance(weights,
cov_matrix)

        results[0,i] = portfolio_return_value
        results[1,i] = portfolio_variance_value
        results[2,i] = results[0,i] / np.sqrt(results[1,i])
```

```
    return results, weights_record
```

```
results,    weights    =    efficient_frontier(expected_returns,
cov_matrix)
```

```
# Plot efficient frontier
plt.figure(figsize=(10, 6))
plt.scatter(results[1,:], results[0,:], c=results[2,:], marker='o')
plt.xlabel('Portfolio Risk (Standard Deviation)')
plt.ylabel('Portfolio Return')
plt.colorbar(label='Sharpe Ratio')
plt.title('Efficient Frontier')
plt.show()
```

Real-World Application: Constructing an Optimal Portfolio

Consider a real-world scenario where you want to construct a portfolio that maximizes the Sharpe Ratio, a measure of risk-adjusted return.

```python
def    negative_sharpe_ratio(weights,    expected_returns,
cov_matrix, risk_free_rate=0.01):
    p_return = portfolio_return(weights, expected_returns)
    p_variance = portfolio_variance(weights, cov_matrix)
    return - (p_return - risk_free_rate) / np.sqrt(p_variance)

def optimize_portfolio_sharpe(expected_returns, cov_matrix,
```

```
risk_free_rate=0.01):
    num_assets = len(expected_returns)
    args = (expected_returns, cov_matrix, risk_free_rate)

    constraints = ({'type': 'eq', 'fun': lambda x: np.sum(x) - 1})
    bounds = tuple((0, 1) for _ in range(num_assets))
    init_guess = num_assets * [1. / num_assets]

    result = minimize(negative_sharpe_ratio, init_guess,
args=args, method='SLSQP', bounds=bounds,
constraints=constraints)

    return result.x

optimal_weights_sharpe                                    =
optimize_portfolio_sharpe(expected_returns, cov_matrix)
print(f"Optimal Weights for Maximum Sharpe Ratio:
{optimal_weights_sharpe}")
```
```

Mean-variance optimization is a powerful technique for constructing an optimal portfolio that balances risk and return. Utilizing Pandas and other Python libraries, you can efficiently compute expected returns, covariance matrices, and optimal asset weights. By understanding and applying these concepts, you can develop sophisticated investment strategies that maximize returns while managing risk effectively.

This comprehensive guide to mean-variance optimization equips you with the knowledge and practical skills necessary to make informed, data-driven investment decisions. By
```

leveraging advanced analytical tools, you can enhance your portfolio management capabilities and achieve superior financial outcomes.

Portfolio Performance Metrics (Sharpe Ratio, Alpha, Beta)

Sharpe Ratio

The Sharpe Ratio, introduced by Nobel laureate William F. Sharpe, measures the risk-adjusted return of a portfolio. It is calculated as the difference between the portfolio return and the risk-free rate, divided by the portfolio's standard deviation (a measure of risk).

$$ \text{Sharpe Ratio} = \frac{R_p - R_f}{\sigma_p} $$

Where:
- R_p is the portfolio return
- R_f is the risk-free rate
- σ_p is the standard deviation of the portfolio returns

To calculate the Sharpe Ratio in Python, start by setting up your environment and importing the necessary libraries:

```bash
pip install pandas numpy
```

```python
```

```
import pandas as pd
import numpy as np

# Example data
returns = pd.Series([0.05, 0.10, -0.02, 0.07, 0.04])
risk_free_rate = 0.01

# Calculate portfolio return and standard deviation
portfolio_return = returns.mean()
portfolio_std_dev = returns.std()

# Calculate Sharpe Ratio
sharpe_ratio    =    (portfolio_return    -    risk_free_rate)    /
portfolio_std_dev
print(f"Sharpe Ratio: {sharpe_ratio}")
```
```

# Alpha

Alpha represents the excess return of a portfolio relative to the return predicted by the Capital Asset Pricing Model (CAPM). It is effectively a measure of how much a portfolio outperforms its expected return, considering its risk (Beta).

$$\alpha = R_p - [R_f + \beta (R_m - R_f)]$$

Where:
- $R_p$ is the portfolio return
- $R_f$ is the risk-free rate
- $\beta$ is the portfolio's beta
```

- \(R_m \) is the market return

To calculate Alpha, you need to estimate the Beta and the expected return based on the market return.

```python
# Example data
market_returns = pd.Series([0.04, 0.08, 0.01, 0.06, 0.03])
portfolio_beta = 1.2

# Calculate market return
market_return = market_returns.mean()

# Calculate expected portfolio return based on CAPM
expected_portfolio_return = risk_free_rate + portfolio_beta * (market_return - risk_free_rate)

# Calculate Alpha
alpha = portfolio_return - expected_portfolio_return
print(f"Alpha: {alpha}")
```

Beta

Beta measures the sensitivity of a portfolio's returns to the returns of the market. A Beta of 1 indicates that the portfolio's price will move with the market. A Beta greater than 1 indicates higher volatility than the market, while a Beta less than 1 indicates lower volatility.

$$\beta = \frac{\text{Cov}(R\_p, R\_m)}{\text{Var}(R\_m)}$$

Where:

- $\text{Cov}(R\_p, R\_m)$ is the covariance between the portfolio returns and the market returns

- $\text{Var}(R\_m)$ is the variance of the market returns

To calculate Beta in Python:

```python
# Calculate covariance matrix
cov_matrix = np.cov(returns, market_returns)

# Calculate Beta
beta = cov_matrix[0, 1] / cov_matrix[1, 1]
print(f"Beta: {beta}")
```

Practical Application with Pandas

Let's apply these concepts with a practical example using historical stock price data. We'll calculate the Sharpe Ratio, Alpha, and Beta for a portfolio of multiple assets.

First, import the necessary libraries and load the historical price data:

```python
import pandas as pd
```

```python
import numpy as np

# Load historical price data
tickers = ['AAPL', 'MSFT', 'GOOG', 'AMZN']
data = pd.DataFrame()

for ticker in tickers:
    data[ticker]          =           pd.read_csv(f'data/{ticker}.csv',
index_col='Date', parse_dates=True)['Adj Close']

# Calculate daily returns
returns = data.pct_change().dropna()
```

Next, calculate the portfolio returns, market returns (using a market index like S&P 500), and the risk-free rate:

```python
# Example market index returns
market_data = pd.read_csv('data/SP500.csv', index_col='Date',
parse_dates=True)['Adj Close']
market_returns = market_data.pct_change().dropna()

# Calculate portfolio returns (equal weighting)
weights = np.array([0.25, 0.25, 0.25, 0.25])
portfolio_returns = returns.dot(weights)

# Set risk-free rate
risk_free_rate = 0.01
```

```
```
```

Calculate the Sharpe Ratio for the portfolio:

```python
portfolio_return = portfolio_returns.mean() * 252 # Annualize
return

portfolio_std_dev = portfolio_returns.std() * np.sqrt(252)  #
Annualize standard deviation

sharpe_ratio   =   (portfolio_return   -   risk_free_rate)   /
portfolio_std_dev
print(f"Sharpe Ratio: {sharpe_ratio}")
```

Calculate Beta for the portfolio:

```python
cov_matrix = np.cov(portfolio_returns, market_returns)
beta = cov_matrix[0, 1] / cov_matrix[1, 1]
print(f"Beta: {beta}")
```

Calculate Alpha for the portfolio:

```python
market_return = market_returns.mean() * 252  # Annualize
market return

expected_portfolio_return   =   risk_free_rate   +   beta   *
(market_return - risk_free_rate)
```
```

```
alpha = portfolio_return - expected_portfolio_return
print(f"Alpha: {alpha}")
```

By mastering these performance metrics, you can gain a deeper understanding of your portfolio's risk and return dynamics. The Sharpe Ratio helps you evaluate the risk-adjusted performance, Alpha measures excess returns relative to a benchmark, and Beta assesses the volatility and market sensitivity of your portfolio. These insights are crucial for making informed investment decisions and optimizing your portfolio's performance.

This comprehensive guide equips you with the theoretical knowledge and practical skills necessary to calculate and interpret key portfolio performance metrics using Python and Pandas. By leveraging these tools, you can enhance your portfolio management capabilities and achieve superior financial outcomes.

Backtesting Trading Strategies

Setting Up Your Environment

To begin backtesting, you need to set up your Python environment with the necessary libraries:

```bash
pip install pandas numpy matplotlib
```

Import the essential libraries:

```python
import pandas as pd
import numpy as np
import matplotlib.pyplot as plt
```

Loading and Preparing Data

For a practical example, let's consider a simple momentum-based trading strategy using historical stock price data. First, load the historical price data:

```python
# Load historical price data
tickers = ['AAPL', 'MSFT', 'GOOG', 'AMZN']
data = pd.DataFrame()

for ticker in tickers:
    data[ticker] = pd.read_csv(f'data/{ticker}.csv', index_col='Date', parse_dates=True)['Adj Close']

# Calculate daily returns
returns = data.pct_change().dropna()
```

Defining the Trading Strategy

A simple momentum strategy involves going long (buying) when the stock price increases over a specific period and short (selling) when the price decreases. Define the strategy parameters and calculate the signals:

```python
# Define momentum window
momentum_window = 20

# Calculate momentum
momentum = data.pct_change(momentum_window)

# Generate trading signals: 1 for buy, -1 for sell
signals = np.where(momentum > 0, 1, -1)
signals = pd.DataFrame(signals, index=data.index, columns=data.columns)
```

Simulating the Strategy

To simulate the strategy, calculate the daily returns of the strategy based on the signals generated:

```python
# Shift the signals to align with the returns
shifted_signals = signals.shift(1)

# Calculate strategy returns
strategy_returns = shifted_signals * returns
```

```python
# Calculate cumulative strategy returns
cumulative_strategy_returns         =         (1         +
strategy_returns).cumprod() - 1

# Calculate cumulative market returns
cumulative_market_returns = (1 + returns).cumprod() - 1
```

Evaluating the Strategy

Evaluate the performance of the strategy by comparing it with the market returns. Plot the cumulative returns to visualize the results:

```python
# Plot cumulative returns
plt.figure(figsize=(14, 7))
plt.plot(cumulative_strategy_returns.mean(axis=1),
label='Strategy Returns')
plt.plot(cumulative_market_returns.mean(axis=1),
label='Market Returns')
plt.title('Cumulative Returns of the Momentum Strategy vs
Market')
plt.xlabel('Date')
plt.ylabel('Cumulative Returns')
plt.legend()
plt.show()
```

Performance Metrics

To gain deeper insights into the strategy's performance, calculate key metrics such as the Sharpe Ratio and maximum drawdown:

```python
# Calculate Sharpe Ratio
risk_free_rate = 0.01
strategy_return = strategy_returns.mean().mean() * 252
strategy_volatility = strategy_returns.std().mean() * np.sqrt(252)
sharpe_ratio = (strategy_return - risk_free_rate) / strategy_volatility
print(f'Sharpe Ratio: {sharpe_ratio}')

# Calculate maximum drawdown
rolling_max = cumulative_strategy_returns.mean(axis=1).cummax()
drawdown = rolling_max - cumulative_strategy_returns.mean(axis=1)
max_drawdown = drawdown.max()
print(f'Maximum Drawdown: {max_drawdown}')
```

Refining the Strategy

Backtesting also provides an opportunity to refine and optimize your strategy. Experiment with different parameters, such as the momentum window, or incorporate additional indicators to enhance performance. For example, combining moving average crossovers with momentum signals can provide a more robust trading signal.

```python
# Define moving averages
short_window = 40
long_window = 100

# Calculate moving averages
signals['short_mavg'] = data.rolling(window=short_window, min_periods=1).mean()
signals['long_mavg'] = data.rolling(window=long_window, min_periods=1).mean()

# Generate trading signals based on moving average crossovers
signals['signal'] = 0.0
signals['signal'][short_window:] = np.where(signals['short_mavg'][short_window:] > signals['long_mavg'][short_window:], 1.0, -1.0)
signals['positions'] = signals['signal'].diff()
```

Practical Application: Case Study

To tie all these concepts together, let's consider a case study using historical data from the S&P 500 index. Suppose you want to validate a momentum-based trading strategy over the past decade. Here's how you could proceed:

1. Load Historical Data: Download S&P 500 historical price data from a reliable source.

2. Define the Strategy: Implement a momentum strategy with a 20-day window.

3. Backtest the Strategy: Calculate the strategy returns and plot cumulative returns against the index.

4. Evaluate Performance: Use performance metrics such as the Sharpe Ratio and maximum drawdown to assess the strategy's effectiveness.

5. Refine the Strategy: Adjust parameters and incorporate additional indicators to enhance performance.

By following these steps, you can systematically evaluate and optimize trading strategies, leveraging the power of Pandas to make data-driven investment decisions. The insights gained from backtesting are invaluable, enabling you to fine-tune your strategies and achieve superior financial outcomes.

Simulating Portfolio Performance Over Time

Setting Up Your Environment

First, ensure you have the necessary libraries installed:

```bash
pip install pandas numpy matplotlib
```

Import the required libraries:

```python
import pandas as pd
import numpy as np
import matplotlib.pyplot as plt
```

Loading and Preparing Data

For this example, let's consider a portfolio composed of four major stocks: Apple (AAPL), Microsoft (MSFT), Google (GOOG), and Amazon (AMZN). Start by loading the historical price data for these stocks:

```python
# Load historical price data
tickers = ['AAPL', 'MSFT', 'GOOG', 'AMZN']
data = pd.DataFrame()

for ticker in tickers:
    data[ticker] = pd.read_csv(f'data/{ticker}.csv', index_col='Date', parse_dates=True)['Adj Close']

# Calculate daily returns
returns = data.pct_change().dropna()
```

Defining Portfolio Weights

Next, define the weights of each stock in your portfolio. For simplicity, we will use equal weights:

```python
# Define portfolio weights
weights = np.array([0.25, 0.25, 0.25, 0.25])
```

Calculating Portfolio Returns

Calculate the daily portfolio returns by multiplying the individual stock returns by their respective weights and summing them up:

```python
# Calculate weighted returns
weighted_returns = returns.mul(weights, axis=1)

# Calculate portfolio returns
portfolio_returns = weighted_returns.sum(axis=1)
```

Simulating Cumulative Portfolio Performance

To simulate the cumulative performance of the portfolio over time, calculate the cumulative returns:

```python
# Calculate cumulative returns
cumulative_returns = (1 + portfolio_returns).cumprod() - 1
```

Visualizing Portfolio Performance

Visualize the cumulative performance of your portfolio using a line plot:

```python
# Plot cumulative portfolio performance
plt.figure(figsize=(14, 7))
plt.plot(cumulative_returns, label='Portfolio Cumulative Returns')
plt.title('Cumulative Portfolio Performance Over Time')
plt.xlabel('Date')
plt.ylabel('Cumulative Returns')
plt.legend()
plt.show()
```

Performance Metrics

To evaluate the portfolio's performance over time, calculate key metrics such as the Sharpe Ratio, maximum drawdown, and annualized returns:

```python
# Calculate annualized returns
annualized_returns = portfolio_returns.mean() * 252

# Calculate annualized volatility
annualized_volatility = portfolio_returns.std() * np.sqrt(252)
```

```python
# Calculate Sharpe Ratio
risk_free_rate = 0.01
sharpe_ratio = (annualized_returns - risk_free_rate) /
annualized_volatility

print(f'Annualized Returns: {annualized_returns:.2%}')
print(f'Annualized Volatility: {annualized_volatility:.2%}')
print(f'Sharpe Ratio: {sharpe_ratio:.2f}')

# Calculate maximum drawdown
rolling_max = cumulative_returns.cummax()
drawdown = rolling_max - cumulative_returns
max_drawdown = drawdown.max()

print(f'Maximum Drawdown: {max_drawdown:.2%}')
```

Stress Testing and Scenario Analysis

To further understand how your portfolio performs under different market conditions, conduct stress tests and scenario analyses. For instance, simulate the portfolio's performance during a market downturn by artificially introducing a significant drop in prices:

```python
# Introduce a market downturn
downturn_factor = 0.7
downturn_returns = portfolio_returns * downturn_factor
```

```
# Calculate cumulative returns during downturn
cumulative_downturn_returns        =        (1        +
downturn_returns).cumprod() - 1

# Plot cumulative returns with downturn
plt.figure(figsize=(14, 7))
plt.plot(cumulative_returns,        label='Original        Portfolio
Cumulative Returns')
plt.plot(cumulative_downturn_returns,        label='Downturn
Portfolio Cumulative Returns', linestyle='--')
plt.title('Cumulative Portfolio Performance with Market
Downturn')
plt.xlabel('Date')
plt.ylabel('Cumulative Returns')
plt.legend()
plt.show()
```
` ` `

Practical Application: Case Study

Let's consider a case study of simulating the performance of an optimized portfolio over the past decade. Assume you have optimized the portfolio based on mean-variance optimization and want to evaluate its historical performance:

1. Load Historical Data: Download historical price data for the selected stocks.

2. Optimize Portfolio Weights: Apply mean-variance optimization to determine the optimal weights.

3. Simulate Performance: Calculate the daily and cumulative portfolio returns based on the optimized weights.

4. Evaluate Performance: Use performance metrics to assess the portfolio's historical performance.

5. Conduct Scenario Analysis: Perform stress tests to evaluate how the portfolio would have performed during market downturns.

Here's an example of how you might implement the optimization and simulation:

```python
from scipy.optimize import minimize

# Calculate covariance matrix of returns
cov_matrix = returns.cov()

# Define objective function for optimization
def portfolio_volatility(weights):
    return np.sqrt(np.dot(weights.T, np.dot(cov_matrix, weights)))

# Set initial weights and constraints
num_assets = len(tickers)
initial_weights = np.ones(num_assets) / num_assets
constraints = ({'type': 'eq', 'fun': lambda weights: np.sum(weights) - 1})
bounds = tuple((0, 1) for _ in range(num_assets))

# Optimize portfolio weights
```

```
optimized_result       =        minimize(portfolio_volatility,
initial_weights,       method='SLSQP',       bounds=bounds,
constraints=constraints)

# Get optimized weights
optimized_weights = optimized_result.x

# Calculate optimized weighted returns
optimized_weighted_returns                                    =
returns.mul(optimized_weights, axis=1)

# Calculate optimized portfolio returns
optimized_portfolio_returns                                   =
optimized_weighted_returns.sum(axis=1)

# Calculate cumulative returns for optimized portfolio
optimized_cumulative_returns         =        (1         +
optimized_portfolio_returns).cumprod() - 1

# Plot optimized cumulative portfolio performance
plt.figure(figsize=(14, 7))
plt.plot(optimized_cumulative_returns,       label='Optimized
Portfolio Cumulative Returns')
plt.title('Cumulative Performance of Optimized Portfolio Over
Time')
plt.xlabel('Date')
plt.ylabel('Cumulative Returns')
plt.legend()
plt.show()
```
```
```

By following these steps, you can effectively simulate and evaluate the performance of your portfolios over time, providing valuable insights for investment decision-making. Leveraging the power of Pandas, you can analyze historical data, optimize portfolios, and conduct detailed performance evaluations to inform your financial strategies.

5.9 Optimization Techniques with Convex Optimization Libraries

Introduction to Convex Optimization

Convex optimization involves solving problems where the objective function is convex, and the feasible region defined by the constraints is also convex. This characteristic ensures that any local minimum is a global minimum, making these problems easier and more reliable to solve.

In finance, convex optimization is commonly used for portfolio optimization, where we seek to balance expected returns against risk. The classic problem is the Markowitz mean-variance optimization, which aims to minimize portfolio variance subject to a target return.

Setting Up the Environment

Before diving into the code, ensure you have the necessary libraries installed. You can do this using pip:

```bash
pip install cvxpy scipy pandas numpy
```

Basic Example: Mean-Variance Optimization

Let's start with a simplified example of mean-variance optimization using CVXPY, a library designed for convex optimization problems.

1. Import Libraries:

```python
import cvxpy as cp
import numpy as np
import pandas as pd
```

2. Generate Synthetic Data:

For illustration, we generate synthetic data representing expected returns and a covariance matrix.

```python
np.random.seed(42)
num_assets = 4
expected_returns = np.random.rand(num_assets)
cov_matrix = np.random.rand(num_assets, num_assets)
cov_matrix = cov_matrix @ cov_matrix.T   # Making it
```

symmetric positive-definite
` ` `

3. Define Variables and Parameters:

```python
weights = cp.Variable(num_assets)
risk = cp.quad_form(weights, cov_matrix)
target_return = cp.Parameter(nonneg=True)
```

4. Formulate the Optimization Problem:

```python
objective = cp.Minimize(risk)
constraints = [cp.sum(weights) == 1, weights >= 0,
expected_returns @ weights >= target_return]
problem = cp.Problem(objective, constraints)
```

5. Solve the Problem:

```python
target_return.value = 0.5  # Example target return
problem.solve()
print("Optimal Weights:", weights.value)
```

This example demonstrates the basics of setting up and

solving a mean-variance optimization problem. The same principles can be extended to more complex scenarios by adjusting the constraints and objective functions.

Advanced Portfolio Optimization

Beyond the basic mean-variance framework, more sophisticated models can be implemented to account for various aspects of portfolio management. Here are some advanced techniques:

1. Risk Parity:

Risk parity aims to allocate capital such that each asset contributes equally to the overall portfolio risk. This can be formulated as a convex optimization problem where the goal is to minimize the difference in risk contributions among assets.

```python
risk_contributions = cp.hstack([cp.quad_form(weights[i], cov_matrix[i, :]) for i in range(num_assets)])
objective = cp.Minimize(cp.norm(risk_contributions - cp.mean(risk_contributions), 2))
constraints = [cp.sum(weights) == 1, weights >= 0]
problem = cp.Problem(objective, constraints)
problem.solve()
print("Risk Parity Weights:", weights.value)
```

2. Minimum CVaR (Conditional Value-at-Risk):

CVaR is a risk measure that considers the tail risk of a portfolio. Minimizing CVaR involves solving a linear programming problem, which can be handled by CVXPY.

```python
alpha = 0.95  # Confidence level
scenarios = np.random.multivariate_normal(expected_returns, cov_matrix, 1000)
portfolio_returns = scenarios @ weights
VaR = np.percentile(portfolio_returns, 100 * (1 - alpha))
CVaR = cp.sum(cp.pos(VaR - portfolio_returns)) / (1000 * (1 - alpha))
objective = cp.Minimize(CVaR)
constraints = [cp.sum(weights) == 1, weights >= 0]
problem = cp.Problem(objective, constraints)
problem.solve()
print("Minimum CVaR Weights:", weights.value)
```

Using SciPy for Optimization

While CVXPY is specifically designed for convex optimization, SciPy's optimization module can also be utilized for solving such problems. Here's an example using SciPy's `minimize` function:

1. Define the Objective Function:

```python
from scipy.optimize import minimize

def portfolio_variance(weights, cov_matrix):
    return weights.T @ cov_matrix @ weights
```

2. Constraints and Initial Guess:

```python
constraints = ({'type': 'eq', 'fun': lambda x: np.sum(x) - 1},
               {'type': 'ineq', 'fun': lambda x: x})
initial_guess = np.ones(num_assets) / num_assets
```

3. Optimize:

```python
result = minimize(portfolio_variance, initial_guess, args=(cov_matrix,), constraints=constraints, method='SLSQP')
print("SciPy Optimal Weights:", result.x)
```

Practical Application: Building an Optimized Portfolio

To bring these concepts into a real-world scenario, let's consider building an optimized portfolio with historical stock data.

1. Fetch Historical Data:

```python
import yfinance as yf

tickers = ['AAPL', 'MSFT', 'GOOGL', 'AMZN']
data = yf.download(tickers, start='2020-01-01',
end='2021-01-01')['Adj Close']
returns = data.pct_change().dropna()
```

2. Calculate Expected Returns and Covariance Matrix:

```python
expected_returns = returns.mean().values
cov_matrix = returns.cov().values
```

3. Optimize Portfolio:

```python
weights = cp.Variable(len(tickers))
risk = cp.quad_form(weights, cov_matrix)
target_return = cp.Parameter(nonneg=True)
objective = cp.Minimize(risk)
constraints = [cp.sum(weights) == 1, weights >= 0,
expected_returns @ weights >= target_return]
problem = cp.Problem(objective, constraints)
```

```
target_return.value = 0.02  # Example target return
problem.solve()
portfolio_weights = pd.Series(weights.value, index=tickers)
print("Optimized Portfolio Weights:", portfolio_weights)
```
` ` `

By applying these optimization techniques, you can construct efficient portfolios, minimize risk, and enhance returns. Remember, the key to mastering financial optimization lies in continuous learning and experimentation with different models and techniques.

5.10 Case Study: Building an Optimized Portfolio

Introduction to the Case Study

Imagine you are a portfolio manager at a financial institution in Vancouver. Your task is to construct a diversified portfolio using a selection of well-known stocks. Your objective is to maximize the portfolio's return while keeping risk at a bay. To achieve this, we'll use historical stock data, perform data cleaning and preprocessing, and apply convex optimization techniques.

Step 1: Fetching Historical Data

First, we need to gather historical stock data for our analysis. We'll use the `yfinance` library to download data for a selection of stocks over a specified period.

1. Install the Necessary Libraries:

```bash
pip install yfinance pandas numpy matplotlib
```

2. Import the Libraries:

```python
import yfinance as yf
import pandas as pd
import numpy as np
import matplotlib.pyplot as plt
```

3. Fetch Historical Data:

We'll download the adjusted closing prices for a set of stocks from January 1, 2020, to January 1, 2021.

```python
tickers = ['AAPL', 'MSFT', 'GOOGL', 'AMZN']
data = yf.download(tickers, start='2020-01-01', end='2021-01-01')['Adj Close']
```

Step 2: Data Cleaning and Preprocessing

Next, we clean and preprocess the data to ensure it's ready for analysis.

1. Calculate Daily Returns:

```python
returns = data.pct_change().dropna()
```

2. Calculate Expected Returns and Covariance Matrix:

```python
expected_returns = returns.mean().values
cov_matrix = returns.cov().values
```

Step 3: Formulating the Optimization Problem

We will use CVXPY to set up and solve the portfolio optimization problem. Our goal is to minimize the portfolio's risk (variance) while achieving a target return.

1. Install CVXPY:

```bash
pip install cvxpy
```

2. Import CVXPY:

```python
```

```python
import cvxpy as cp
```

3. Define Variables and Parameters:

```python
num_assets = len(tickers)
weights = cp.Variable(num_assets)
risk = cp.quad_form(weights, cov_matrix)
target_return = cp.Parameter(nonneg=True)
```

4. Formulate the Optimization Problem:

```python
objective = cp.Minimize(risk)
constraints = [cp.sum(weights) == 1, weights >= 0,
expected_returns @ weights >= target_return]
problem = cp.Problem(objective, constraints)
```

Step 4: Solving the Optimization Problem

We will solve the optimization problem for a specific target return and obtain the optimal weights for the portfolio.

1. Set Target Return and Solve:

```python
```

```python
target_return.value = 0.02  # Example target return of 2%
problem.solve()
```

2. Retrieve Optimal Weights:

```python
optimal_weights = pd.Series(weights.value, index=tickers)
print("Optimized Portfolio Weights:", optimal_weights)
```

Step 5: Portfolio Performance Analysis

With the optimized weights, we can analyze the portfolio's performance and visualize the results.

1. Calculate Portfolio Returns:

```python
portfolio_returns = returns.dot(optimal_weights)
```

2. Plot Cumulative Returns:

```python
cumulative_returns = (1 + portfolio_returns).cumprod()
cumulative_returns.plot(figsize=(10, 6), title="Optimized Portfolio Cumulative Returns")
plt.show()
```

```
` ` `
```

Step 6: Advanced Optimization Techniques

To further enhance our portfolio, we can explore advanced optimization techniques such as risk parity and minimum CVaR.

1. Risk Parity Optimization:

```python
risk_contributions = cp.hstack([cp.quad_form(weights[i], cov_matrix[i, :]) for i in range(num_assets)])
objective = cp.Minimize(cp.norm(risk_contributions - cp.mean(risk_contributions), 2))
constraints = [cp.sum(weights) == 1, weights >= 0]
problem = cp.Problem(objective, constraints)
problem.solve()
risk_parity_weights = pd.Series(weights.value, index=tickers)
print("Risk Parity Weights:", risk_parity_weights)
```

2. Minimum CVaR Optimization:

```python
alpha = 0.95  # Confidence level
scenarios = np.random.multivariate_normal(expected_returns, cov_matrix, 1000)
```

```python
portfolio_returns = scenarios @ weights
VaR = np.percentile(portfolio_returns, 100 * (1 - alpha))
CVaR = cp.sum(cp.pos(VaR - portfolio_returns)) / (1000 * (1 - alpha))
objective = cp.Minimize(CVaR)
constraints = [cp.sum(weights) == 1, weights >= 0]
problem = cp.Problem(objective, constraints)
problem.solve()
cvar_weights = pd.Series(weights.value, index=tickers)
print("Minimum CVaR Weights:", cvar_weights)
```

Step 7: Real-World Application and Reporting

Finally, we apply our optimized portfolio to real-world scenarios and generate a comprehensive report.

1. Generate Report:

```python
report = pd.DataFrame({
    'Stock': tickers,
    'Optimized Weights': optimal_weights,
    'Risk Parity Weights': risk_parity_weights,
    'Minimum CVaR Weights': cvar_weights
})
print(report)
```

2. Discuss Findings:

Analyze the performance of each optimized portfolio and discuss insights, such as the balance between risk and return, diversification benefits, and potential areas for improvement.

By following this detailed case study, you now have a practical understanding of how to build an optimized portfolio using advanced Pandas techniques and convex optimization libraries. This hands-on approach not only reinforces theoretical knowledge but also equips you with the skills to apply these concepts in real-world financial analysis.

CHAPTER 5: RISK MANAGEMENT AND FINANCIAL METRICS

V olatility reflects the uncertainty or risk associated with the price changes of an asset. High volatility means that the price of the asset can change drastically over a short period, while low volatility indicates more stable price movements. For financial analysts, accurately measuring and analyzing volatility is crucial for risk management, portfolio optimization, and trading strategies.

Step 1: Fetching Historical Data

To start, we need to gather historical price data for the assets we are analyzing. We'll use the `yfinance` library to download the adjusted closing prices for a set of stocks.

1. Install Necessary Libraries:

```bash
pip install yfinance pandas numpy matplotlib
```

` ` `

2. Import the Libraries:

```python
import yfinance as yf
import pandas as pd
import numpy as np
import matplotlib.pyplot as plt
```

3. Fetch Historical Data:

We'll download the adjusted closing prices for a set of stocks from January 1, 2020, to January 1, 2021.

```python
tickers = ['AAPL', 'MSFT', 'GOOGL', 'AMZN']
data = yf.download(tickers, start='2020-01-01', end='2021-01-01')['Adj Close']
```

Step 2: Calculating Daily Returns

Daily returns are essential for measuring volatility as they show the percentage change in an asset's price from one day to the next.

1. Calculate Daily Returns:

```python
returns = data.pct_change().dropna()
```

Step 3: Calculating Historical Volatility

Historical volatility is the standard deviation of the asset's returns over a specific period. It provides a measure of the asset's past price fluctuations.

1. Calculate Historical Volatility:

```python
volatility = returns.std() * np.sqrt(252)   # Annualized volatility
print("Historical Volatility:", volatility)
```

Here, we annualize the daily standard deviation by multiplying it by the square root of the number of trading days in a year (approximately 252).

Step 4: Visualizing Volatility

Visualization helps in understanding the volatility trends and patterns over time. We'll plot the rolling volatility of the asset returns.

1. Calculate Rolling Volatility:

```python
rolling_volatility = returns.rolling(window=21).std() * np.sqrt(252)
```

2. Plot Rolling Volatility:

```python
rolling_volatility.plot(figsize=(10, 6), title="Rolling 21-Day Volatility")
plt.xlabel('Date')
plt.ylabel('Volatility')
plt.show()
```

Step 5: Advanced Volatility Measures

While historical volatility provides a basic measure, advanced techniques offer a more nuanced understanding of market risk. We will explore two such methods: Exponentially Weighted Moving Average (EWMVolatility and GARCH (Generalized Autoregressive Conditional Heteroskedasticity) Volatility.

Exponentially Weighted Moving Average (EWMVolatility

EWMA volatility gives more weight to recent observations, making it more responsive to recent market changes.

1. Calculate EWMA Volatility:

```python
lambda_ = 0.94
ewma_volatility          =          returns.ewm(span=(2/(1-lambda_))).std().dropna() * np.sqrt(252)
```

2. Plot EWMA Volatility:

```python
ewma_volatility.plot(figsize=(10,     6),     title="EWMA Volatility")
plt.xlabel('Date')
plt.ylabel('Volatility')
plt.show()
```

GARCH Volatility

GARCH models are used to estimate volatility by considering both past squared returns and past variances. We'll use the `arch` library for this purpose.

1. Install the ARCH Library:

```bash
pip install arch
```

2. Import the ARCH Library:

```python
from arch import arch_model
```

3. Fit a GARCH Model:

```python
model = arch_model(returns['AAPL'], vol='Garch', p=1, q=1)
garch_results = model.fit()
```

4. Extract and Plot GARCH Volatility:

```python
garch_volatility = garch_results.conditional_volatility * np.sqrt(252)
garch_volatility.plot(figsize=(10, 6), title="GARCH Volatility")
plt.xlabel('Date')
plt.ylabel('Volatility')
plt.show()
```

Step 6: Real-World Application and Interpretation

Understanding the different measures of volatility and their implications is crucial for practical financial analysis. Here, we will interpret the results and discuss their applications.

1. Historical Volatility:

Historical volatility provides a straightforward measure of past price fluctuations, useful for risk estimation and portfolio diversification.

2. Rolling Volatility:

Rolling volatility helps in identifying periods of high and low volatility, crucial for timing market entries and exits.

3. EWMA Volatility:

EWMA volatility's responsiveness to recent data makes it ideal for dynamic risk management strategies.

4. GARCH Volatility:

GARCH models capture volatility clustering and provide forecasts, essential for derivative pricing and risk management.

Measuring and analyzing volatility is a multifaceted process requiring various techniques to capture different aspects of market risk. By leveraging Pandas and other Python libraries, financial analysts can perform sophisticated volatility analysis, enabling informed decision-making and robust risk management. Through this comprehensive approach, you gain a deeper understanding of market dynamics, enhancing your ability to navigate the complexities of financial markets.

Value-at-Risk (VaR) Calculations

VaR quantifies the maximum expected loss over a specified time period within a given confidence interval. For instance, if a portfolio has a one-day VaR of $1 million at a 95% confidence level, it means there is a 5% chance the portfolio will lose more than $1 million in a single day. VaR is widely used in risk management, financial reporting, and regulatory compliance.

Step 1: Fetching Historical Data

To perform VaR calculations, we first need historical price data. We'll use the `yfinance` library to download the adjusted closing prices for a set of stocks.

1. Install Necessary Libraries:

```bash
pip install yfinance pandas numpy scipy matplotlib
```

2. Import the Libraries:

```python
import yfinance as yf
import pandas as pd
import numpy as np
import scipy.stats as stats
import matplotlib.pyplot as plt
```

3. Fetch Historical Data:

We'll download the adjusted closing prices for a set of stocks from January 1, 2020, to January 1, 2021.

```python
tickers = ['AAPL', 'MSFT', 'GOOGL', 'AMZN']
data = yf.download(tickers, start='2020-01-01', end='2021-01-01')['Adj Close']
```

Step 2: Calculating Daily Returns

Daily returns are essential for VaR calculations as they show the percentage change in an asset's price from one day to the next.

1. Calculate Daily Returns:

```python
returns = data.pct_change().dropna()
```

Step 3: Parametric VaR Calculation

Parametric VaR, also known as variance-covariance VaR, assumes that returns follow a normal distribution. This method calculates VaR using the mean and standard deviation of the portfolio returns.

1. Calculate Portfolio Mean and Standard Deviation:

```python
portfolio_mean = returns.mean().mean()
portfolio_std = returns.std().mean()
```

2. Calculate VaR at 95% Confidence Level:

```python
confidence_level = 0.95
z_score = stats.norm.ppf(confidence_level)
VaR_95 = portfolio_mean - z_score * portfolio_std
print("Parametric VaR (95%):", VaR_95)
```

Step 4: Historical VaR Calculation

Historical VaR involves sorting historical returns and selecting the percentile corresponding to the desired confidence level. This method does not assume any distribution and uses actual historical data.

1. Calculate Historical VaR:

```python
VaR_95_hist = returns.quantile(1 - confidence_level)
print("Historical VaR (95%):", VaR_95_hist)
```

Step 5: Monte Carlo Simulation VaR

Monte Carlo simulation involves generating a large number of random price paths based on historical returns and calculating the potential losses. This method provides a flexible and robust approach to VaR estimation.

1. Generate Random Price Paths:

```python
num_simulations = 10000
simulated_returns = np.random.normal(portfolio_mean, portfolio_std, num_simulations)
```

2. Calculate Simulated VaR:

```python
VaR_95_mc = -np.percentile(simulated_returns, (1 - confidence_level) * 100)
print("Monte Carlo VaR (95%):", VaR_95_m
```

Step 6: Visualizing VaR

Visualization helps in understanding the distribution of returns and the calculated VaR. We'll plot the histogram of returns along with the VaR threshold.

1. Plot Histogram of Returns:

```python
```

```
plt.figure(figsize=(10, 6))

plt.hist(returns, bins=50, alpha=0.7, label='Returns')

plt.axvline(x=VaR_95, color='r', linestyle='--', linewidth=2,
label='Parametric VaR (95%)')

plt.axvline(x=VaR_95_hist.mean(), color='g', linestyle='--',
linewidth=2, label='Historical VaR (95%)')

plt.axvline(x=-VaR_95_mc, color='b', linestyle='--',
linewidth=2, label='Monte Carlo VaR (95%)')

plt.xlabel('Returns')

plt.ylabel('Frequency')

plt.title('Distribution of Returns and VaR')

plt.legend()

plt.show()
```
``` `

Step 7: Real-World Application and Interpretation

Understanding and interpreting VaR results is crucial for practical risk management. Here, we will interpret the results and discuss their applications.

1. Parametric VaR:

Parametric VaR is straightforward to calculate but relies heavily on the assumption of normal distribution, which may not always hold true in financial returns.

2. Historical VaR:

Historical VaR is model-independent and uses actual
```

historical data, making it more realistic but limited by the historical dataset's size and relevance.

3. Monte Carlo VaR:

Monte Carlo VaR provides a flexible and robust approach, capable of capturing more complex return distributions, but it is computationally intensive.

Calculating and interpreting VaR is essential for understanding and managing financial risk. By leveraging Pandas and other Python libraries, financial analysts can perform sophisticated VaR analysis, enabling informed decision-making and robust risk management. Through this comprehensive approach, you gain a deeper understanding of market risk, enhancing your ability to navigate the complexities of financial markets.

Conditional Value-at-Risk (CVaR) Calculations

Introduction to Conditional Value-at-Risk (CVaR)

CVaR is designed to address some of the limitations of VaR by considering the tail-end of the loss distribution. It provides a more robust measure of risk by averaging the worst losses beyond the VaR cut-off. This makes CVaR particularly useful for understanding the potential impact of extreme market events.

Step 1: Fetching Historical Data

As with VaR calculations, we start by obtaining historical

price data. We'll use the `yfinance` library to download the adjusted closing prices for a set of stocks.

1. Install Necessary Libraries:

```bash
pip install yfinance pandas numpy scipy matplotlib
```

2. Import the Libraries:

```python
import yfinance as yf
import pandas as pd
import numpy as np
import scipy.stats as stats
import matplotlib.pyplot as plt
```

3. Fetch Historical Data:

We'll download the adjusted closing prices for a set of stocks from January 1, 2020, to January 1, 2021.

```python
tickers = ['AAPL', 'MSFT', 'GOOGL', 'AMZN']
data = yf.download(tickers, start='2020-01-01', end='2021-01-01')['Adj Close']
```

Step 2: Calculating Daily Returns

Daily returns are essential for CVaR calculations as they show the percentage change in an asset's price from one day to the next.

1. Calculate Daily Returns:

```python
returns = data.pct_change().dropna()
```

Step 3: Calculating Value-at-Risk (VaR)

Before calculating CVaR, we need to determine the VaR. We'll use the historical method in this example.

1. Calculate Historical VaR:

```python
confidence_level = 0.95
VaR_95 = returns.quantile(1 - confidence_level)
```

Step 4: Calculating Conditional Value-at-Risk (CVaR)

CVaR is the average of the losses that exceed the VaR threshold. We'll filter the returns to include only those that are less than or equal to the VaR and then calculate the mean of these returns.

1. Calculate CVaR:

```python
CVaR_95 = returns[returns <= VaR_95].mean()
print("CVaR (95%):", CVaR_95)
```

Step 5: Visualizing CVaR

Visualization aids in understanding the distribution of returns and the calculated CVaR. We'll plot the histogram of returns along with the VaR and CVaR thresholds.

1. Plot Histogram of Returns:

```python
plt.figure(figsize=(10, 6))
plt.hist(returns, bins=50, alpha=0.7, label='Returns')
plt.axvline(x=VaR_95.mean(), color='r', linestyle='--', linewidth=2, label='VaR (95%)')
plt.axvline(x=CVaR_95.mean(), color='g', linestyle='--', linewidth=2, label='CVaR (95%)')
plt.xlabel('Returns')
plt.ylabel('Frequency')
plt.title('Distribution of Returns and CVaR')
plt.legend()
plt.show()
```

Step 6: Real-World Application and Interpretation

Understanding and interpreting CVaR results is crucial for practical risk management. Here, we will interpret the results and discuss their applications.

1. Enhanced Risk Assessment:

CVaR provides a more comprehensive view of risk by considering tail-end losses. This makes it especially useful for risk management in volatile markets where extreme events can have significant impacts.

2. Portfolio Allocation:

By incorporating CVaR into portfolio allocation decisions, financial analysts can better manage and mitigate the risks associated with extreme market movements.

3. Regulatory Compliance:

Many financial regulators and institutions prefer CVaR over VaR due to its robustness in capturing extreme risks, making it a valuable metric for regulatory reporting and compliance.

Calculating and interpreting CVaR is essential for a more nuanced understanding of financial risk. By leveraging Pandas and other Python libraries, financial analysts can perform sophisticated CVaR analysis, enabling informed decision-making and robust risk management. Through this comprehensive approach, you gain a deeper understanding of market risk, enhancing your ability to navigate the complexities of financial markets.

6.4 Stress Testing and Scenario Analysis

Introduction to Stress Testing and Scenario Analysis

Stress testing involves simulating extreme market conditions to evaluate the impact on financial assets or portfolios. Meanwhile, scenario analysis encompasses examining various hypothetical situations to understand potential risks and opportunities. Together, these methods provide a comprehensive view of how portfolios might behave under adverse conditions, aiding in proactive risk management.

Step 1: Setting Up the Environment

Before diving into the analysis, we need to set up our Python environment with the necessary libraries.

1. Install Required Libraries:

```bash
pip install yfinance pandas numpy matplotlib
```

2. Import Libraries:

```python
import yfinance as yf
```

```python
import pandas as pd
import numpy as np
import matplotlib.pyplot as plt
```

Step 2: Fetching Historical Data

To perform stress testing and scenario analysis, we first need historical price data for the assets in our portfolio.

1. Download Historical Data:

Let's fetch the adjusted closing prices for a set of stocks from January 1, 2020, to January 1, 2021.

```python
tickers = ['AAPL', 'MSFT', 'GOOGL', 'AMZN']
data = yf.download(tickers, start='2020-01-01', end='2021-01-01')['Adj Close']
```

Step 3: Calculating Daily Returns

Daily returns are essential for understanding the historical performance of assets and simulating future scenarios.

1. Calculate Daily Returns:

```python
returns = data.pct_change().dropna()
```

```
` ` `
```

Step 4: Defining Stress Testing Scenarios

Stress testing involves defining extreme scenarios that could potentially impact the portfolio. Common stress scenarios include market crashes, interest rate spikes, and geopolitical events.

1. Market Crash Scenario:

Simulate a market crash by assuming a sudden 20% drop in stock prices.

```python
crash_scenario = returns.apply(lambda x: x - 0.20)
```

2. Interest Rate Spike Scenario:

Simulate an interest rate spike by assuming a 2% increase in interest rates, affecting interest-sensitive stocks.

```python
rate_spike_scenario = returns.apply(lambda x: x - 0.02 if 'interest_sensitive' in x.name else x)
```

Step 5: Applying Stress Scenarios to the Portfolio

We apply the defined stress scenarios to the portfolio to

evaluate the potential impact.

1. Apply Market Crash Scenario:

```python
portfolio_value_crash = (1 + crash_scenario).cumprod().iloc[-1]
print("Portfolio Value after Market Crash:", portfolio_value_crash)
```

2. Apply Interest Rate Spike Scenario:

```python
portfolio_value_rate_spike = (1 + rate_spike_scenario).cumprod().iloc[-1]
print("Portfolio Value after Interest Rate Spike:", portfolio_value_rate_spike)
```

Step 6: Visualizing Stress Test Results

Visualization helps in understanding the impact of stress scenarios on the portfolio. We'll use Matplotlib to plot the portfolio's performance under different scenarios.

1. Plot Portfolio Performance:

```python
plt.figure(figsize=(10, 6))
```

```
plt.plot((1 + returns).cumprod(), label='Original Portfolio')
plt.plot((1 + crash_scenario).cumprod(), label='Market Crash
Scenario', linestyle='--')
plt.plot((1 + rate_spike_scenario).cumprod(), label='Interest
Rate Spike Scenario', linestyle='--')
plt.xlabel('Date')
plt.ylabel('Portfolio Value')
plt.title('Portfolio Performance under Stress Scenarios')
plt.legend()
plt.show()
```

Step 7: Scenario Analysis

Scenario analysis involves creating hypothetical situations to evaluate the potential outcomes. Unlike stress testing, which focuses on extreme events, scenario analysis can include both positive and negative scenarios.

1. Define Custom Scenarios:

Let's create a custom scenario where we assume a gradual 10% increase in stock prices.

```python
custom_scenario = returns.apply(lambda x: x + 0.10)
```

2. Apply Custom Scenario:

```python
portfolio_value_custom = (1 +
custom_scenario).cumprod().iloc[-1]

print("Portfolio Value after Custom Scenario:",
portfolio_value_custom)
```

Step 8: Interpreting Results

The ultimate goal of stress testing and scenario analysis is to derive actionable insights.

1. Risk Mitigation:

If the portfolio shows significant vulnerability under certain stress scenarios, it may indicate the need for diversification or hedging strategies.

2. Strategic Adjustments:

Scenario analysis can reveal opportunities for strategic adjustments. For instance, a positive custom scenario might suggest increasing exposure to certain sectors.

3. Regulatory Compliance:

Stress testing results are often required for regulatory compliance, ensuring that financial institutions are prepared for adverse market conditions.

Stress testing and scenario analysis are indispensable

tools for comprehensive risk management. By simulating extreme market conditions and hypothetical scenarios, financial analysts can anticipate potential impacts, identify vulnerabilities, and formulate effective risk mitigation strategies. Leveraging the power of Pandas and other Python libraries, you can perform sophisticated stress testing and scenario analysis, enhancing your ability to navigate the complexities of financial markets.

Drawdown Analysis

A drawdown is defined as the peak-to-trough decline during a specific period of an investment, portfolio, or fund. It is expressed as a percentage between the peak and the subsequent trough. Drawdowns are significant as they provide insights into the risk exposure of an investment, helping investors make informed decisions about capital allocation and risk mitigation.

Step 1: Setting Up the Environment

To begin with, let's ensure our Python environment is ready with the necessary libraries.

1. Install Required Libraries:

```bash
pip install yfinance pandas numpy matplotlib
```

2. Import Libraries:

```python
import yfinance as yf
import pandas as pd
import numpy as np
import matplotlib.pyplot as plt
```

Step 2: Fetching Historical Data

We need historical price data to calculate drawdowns. For this example, we will download the adjusted closing prices of a few stocks.

1. Download Historical Data:

```python
tickers = ['AAPL', 'MSFT', 'GOOGL', 'AMZN']
data    =    yf.download(tickers,    start='2020-01-01', end='2021-01-01')['Adj Close']
```

Step 3: Calculating Cumulative Returns

Cumulative returns provide a basis for measuring drawdowns. The process involves calculating the daily returns and then computing the cumulative product of those returns.

1. Calculate Daily Returns:

```python
returns = data.pct_change().dropna()
```

2. Calculate Cumulative Returns:

```python
cumulative_returns = (1 + returns).cumprod()
```

Step 4: Identifying Peak Values

To analyze drawdowns, we need to identify the peak values in the cumulative returns series. These peaks represent the highest points before the drawdowns begin.

1. Calculate Rolling Maximum:

```python
rolling_max = cumulative_returns.cummax()
```

Step 5: Calculating Drawdowns

Drawdowns can now be calculated by comparing the cumulative returns to their respective rolling maximum values. The difference, expressed as a percentage, represents the drawdown.

1. Calculate Drawdowns:

```python
drawdowns = cumulative_returns / rolling_max - 1
```

Step 6: Visualizing Drawdowns

Visualization is a powerful tool for understanding the periods and severity of drawdowns. We will use Matplotlib to create a clear visual representation.

1. Plot Drawdowns:

```python
plt.figure(figsize=(10, 6))
plt.plot(drawdowns, label='Drawdown')
plt.fill_between(drawdowns.index,        drawdowns.min(),
drawdowns, color='red', alpha=0.3)
plt.xlabel('Date')
plt.ylabel('Drawdown')
plt.title('Drawdown Analysis')
plt.legend()
plt.show()
```

Step 7: Analyzing Drawdown Metrics

To gain deeper insights, we can calculate specific drawdown metrics, such as the maximum drawdown and the duration of drawdowns.

1. Calculate Maximum Drawdown:

```python
max_drawdown = drawdowns.min()
print("Maximum Drawdown:", max_drawdown)
```

2. Calculate Drawdown Duration:

Drawdown duration is the time taken for the portfolio to recover from a drawdown. It can be measured using the following code:

```python
drawdown_duration = (drawdowns == 0).astype(int).groupby(drawdowns.ne(0).astype(int).cumsum()).cumsum()
max_drawdown_duration = drawdown_duration.max()
print("Maximum Drawdown Duration:", max_drawdown_duration)
```

Step 8: Interpreting Drawdown Analysis

Understanding the implications of drawdown analysis is vital for making informed investment decisions.

1. Risk Assessment:

A high maximum drawdown indicates higher risk, which

might be unacceptable for conservative investors. Conversely, a lower drawdown suggests a more stable investment.

2. Investment Strategy Evaluation:

Drawdown duration provides insights into the recovery period of investments. Strategies with prolonged recovery periods may require reassessment.

3. Portfolio Adjustment:

If drawdown analysis reveals significant vulnerabilities, it might prompt reallocating assets or diversifying investments to enhance resilience.

4. Performance Benchmarking:

Comparing drawdowns of different portfolios or benchmarks helps in evaluating relative performance and risk-adjusted returns.

Drawdown analysis is a cornerstone of risk management, providing a clear view of the potential losses and recovery periods in a portfolio. By utilizing the Pandas library, financial analysts can efficiently calculate and visualize drawdowns, gaining valuable insights into the risk profile of their investments. This analysis not only aids in risk assessment but also informs strategic adjustments to enhance portfolio resilience.

Credit Risk Analysis

Credit risk analysis involves evaluating the likelihood that a borrower will default on their debt and the potential loss severity if a default occurs. Key metrics in credit risk analysis include the Probability of Default (PD), Loss Given Default (LGD), and Exposure at Default (EAD). By analyzing these components, financial professionals can better gauge the creditworthiness of borrowers and make informed lending or investment decisions.

Step 1: Setting Up the Environment

To begin our analysis, we need to prepare our Python environment with the necessary libraries.

1. Install Required Libraries:

```bash
pip install pandas numpy yfinance scikit-learn
```

2. Import Libraries:

```python
import pandas as pd
import numpy as np
import yfinance as yf
from sklearn.linear_model import LogisticRegression
from sklearn.model_selection import train_test_split
from sklearn.metrics import classification_report, roc_auc_score
```

```
` ` `
```

Step 2: Gathering and Preparing Data

Credit risk analysis requires historical financial data on borrowers, including their credit history, financial statements, and macroeconomic indicators. For this example, we will simulate a dataset representing various financial metrics of borrowers.

1. Simulate Borrower Data:

```python
np.random.seed(42)
data = pd.DataFrame({
    'age': np.random.randint(21, 70, size=1000),
    'income':        np.random.uniform(30000,        120000,
size=1000),
    'loan_amount':   np.random.uniform(5000,        50000,
size=1000),
    'loan_term': np.random.randint(12, 60, size=1000),
    'credit_score': np.random.uniform(300, 850, size=1000),
    'defaulted': np.random.choice([0, 1], size=1000, p=[0.9,
0.1])
})
```

Step 3: Exploratory Data Analysis (EDA)

Exploratory Data Analysis helps us understand the

characteristics of our dataset, identify patterns, and detect anomalies.

1. Summary Statistics:

```python
print(data.describe())
```

2. Visualize Data Distribution:

```python
import matplotlib.pyplot as plt
import seaborn as sns

sns.pairplot(data, hue='defaulted')
plt.show()
```

Step 4: Feature Engineering

Feature engineering involves creating new features or transforming existing ones to improve the predictive power of our model.

1. Calculate Debt-to-Income Ratio:

```python
data['dti_ratio'] = data['loan_amount'] / data['income']
```

2. Categorize Credit Scores:

```python
def categorize_credit_score(score):
    if score < 580:
        return 'poor'
    elif score < 670:
        return 'fair'
    elif score < 740:
        return 'good'
    else:
        return 'excellent'

data['credit_category']                                    =
data['credit_score'].apply(categorize_credit_score)
```

Step 5: Building Predictive Models

We will use logistic regression to predict the probability of default based on the financial metrics of borrowers.

1. Split Data into Training and Testing Sets:

```python
X = data[['age', 'income', 'loan_amount', 'loan_term',
'dti_ratio']]
y = data['defaulted']
```

```
X_train, X_test, y_train, y_test = train_test_split(X, y,
test_size=0.3, random_state=42)
```

2. Train Logistic Regression Model:

```python
model = LogisticRegression()
model.fit(X_train, y_train)
```

3. Evaluate Model Performance:

```python
y_pred = model.predict(X_test)
y_prob = model.predict_proba(X_test)[:, 1]

print(classification_report(y_test, y_pred))
print("ROC AUC Score:", roc_auc_score(y_test, y_prob))
```

Step 6: Calculating Credit Risk Metrics

We can now calculate key credit risk metrics using the trained model.

1. Probability of Default (PD):

Probability of Default is calculated as the predicted probability of a borrower defaulting on their loan.

```python
data['probability_of_default']                    =
model.predict_proba(data[['age',   'income',   'loan_amount',
'loan_term', 'dti_ratio']])[:, 1]
```

2. Loss Given Default (LGD):

Loss Given Default estimates the percentage of exposure that would be lost if a borrower defaults. For simplicity, let's assume a fixed recovery rate of 40%.

```python
recovery_rate = 0.40
data['loss_given_default']  =  data['loan_amount']  *  (1  -
recovery_rate)
```

3. Exposure at Default (EAD):

Exposure at Default represents the total amount of exposure at the time of default. Here, we assume that the full loan amount is at risk.

```python
data['exposure_at_default'] = data['loan_amount']
```

Step 7: Visualizing Credit Risk

Visualizations help to communicate the findings of our credit risk analysis effectively.

1. Plot Probability of Default:

```python
plt.figure(figsize=(10, 6))
sns.histplot(data['probability_of_default'],           bins=50,
kde=True)
plt.xlabel('Probability of Default')
plt.ylabel('Frequency')
plt.title('Distribution of Probability of Default')
plt.show()
```

2. Plot Loss Given Default:

```python
plt.figure(figsize=(10, 6))
sns.histplot(data['loss_given_default'], bins=50, kde=True,
color='red')
plt.xlabel('Loss Given Default')
plt.ylabel('Frequency')
plt.title('Distribution of Loss Given Default')
plt.show()
```

Step 8: Interpreting Credit Risk Analysis

Interpreting the results of credit risk analysis is critical for making informed financial decisions.

1. Risk Segmentation:

Borrowers can be segmented based on their probability of default and credit risk metrics, allowing for targeted risk management strategies.

2. Loan Pricing:

Lenders can use credit risk metrics to set interest rates that reflect the risk profile of borrowers, ensuring adequate compensation for the risk taken.

3. Portfolio Management:

By analyzing the aggregate credit risk of a portfolio, financial institutions can make strategic adjustments to maintain a balanced risk-return profile.

4. Regulatory Compliance:

Accurate credit risk analysis helps institutions comply with regulatory requirements, such as those outlined in Basel III, which mandate robust risk assessment and capital adequacy measures.

Credit risk analysis is a fundamental aspect of financial risk management, enabling lenders and investors to assess the likelihood and impact of borrower defaults. Utilizing the Pandas library, we can efficiently perform credit risk analysis, from data preparation and feature engineering to predictive modeling and visualization. This comprehensive approach equips financial professionals with the insights needed to manage credit risk effectively and make informed decisions.

Profit and Loss Attribution

P&L attribution provides a detailed breakdown of the returns of a portfolio. It helps identify whether the performance is due to market movements, asset selection, sector allocation, or other factors. Understanding these components is essential for financial analysts and portfolio managers who must justify their investment decisions and communicate effectively with stakeholders.

Key Components of P&L Attribution

1. Market Return Contribution: The portion of the portfolio's return that is attributed to the overall market movement.

2. Sector Allocation: The impact of having a higher or lower exposure to various sectors compared to a benchmark.

3. Security Selection: The effect of choosing specific securities within each sector.

4. Currency Effects: The influence of foreign exchange movements on the portfolio's return.

5. Interest Rate Effects: The impact of changes in interest rates, particularly relevant for fixed income portfolios.

Step-by-Step Guide to P&L Attribution Using Pandas

1. Data Preparation

The first step in P&L attribution involves gathering and preparing the financial data. This includes historical prices, returns, sector classifications, and benchmarks. Pandas make it easy to handle large datasets and perform the necessary data transformations.

```python
import pandas as pd

# Load historical price data
prices = pd.read_csv('historical_prices.csv', parse_dates=['Date'], index_col='Date')

# Load sector classification
sectors = pd.read_csv('sector_classification.csv')

# Merge datasets
data = pd.merge(prices, sectors, on='Security')
```

2. Calculating Returns

Next, calculate the daily returns for each security in the portfolio. This step is crucial as it forms the basis for further analysis.

```python
# Calculate daily returns
data['Return'] = data.groupby('Security')['Price'].pct_change()
```

3. Market Return Contribution

To isolate the market return contribution, compare the portfolio's returns with a benchmark index.

```python
# Load benchmark data
benchmark = pd.read_csv('benchmark_prices.csv', parse_dates=['Date'], index_col='Date')
benchmark['Return'] = benchmark['Price'].pct_change()

# Calculate market return contribution
data['Market_Contribution'] = data['Return'] - benchmark['Return']
```

4. Sector Allocation Attribution

Analyze the effect of sector allocations by comparing the sector weights of the portfolio to those of the benchmark.

```python
# Calculate sector weights
sector_weights = data.groupby(['Date', 'Sector'])['Market Value'].sum() / data.groupby('Date')['Market Value'].sum()
benchmark_weights = benchmark.groupby(['Date', 'Sector'])['Market Value'].sum() / benchmark.groupby('Date')['Market Value'].sum()

# Calculate sector allocation effect
```

```python
data['Sector_Allocation_Effect']   =   (sector_weights   -
benchmark_weights) * benchmark.groupby(['Date', 'Sector'])
['Return'].mean()
```

5. Security Selection Attribution

Evaluate the impact of selecting specific securities within each sector.

```python
# Calculate security selection effect
data['Security_Selection_Effect']   =   data.groupby('Sector')
['Return'].mean()        -        benchmark.groupby('Sector')
['Return'].mean()
```

6. Currency and Interest Rate Effects

For portfolios with international exposure, account for currency effects. Similarly, for fixed income portfolios, consider the impact of interest rate changes.

```python
# Load currency and interest rate data
currency_data       =       pd.read_csv('currency_data.csv',
parse_dates=['Date'], index_col='Date')

interest_rate_data   =   pd.read_csv('interest_rate_data.csv',
parse_dates=['Date'], index_col='Date')

# Calculate currency effect
```

```python
data['Currency_Effect']          =          data['Return']          -
currency_data['FX_Rate'].pct_change()
```

```
# Calculate interest rate effect
data['Interest_Rate_Effect']          =          data['Return']          -
interest_rate_data['Interest_Rate'].pct_change()
```

7. Summarizing P&L Attribution

Finally, bring together all the components of P&L attribution into a comprehensive summary.

```python
# Summarize P&L attribution
summary = data.groupby('Date').agg({
    'Market_Contribution': 'sum',
    'Sector_Allocation_Effect': 'sum',
    'Security_Selection_Effect': 'sum',
    'Currency_Effect': 'sum',
    'Interest_Rate_Effect': 'sum'
})

# Display summary
print(summary)
```

Practical Example: A Case Study

Imagine you are managing a diversified equity portfolio. You've observed a performance deviation from the benchmark over the last quarter. Using the steps outlined, you can attribute this deviation to specific factors:

1. Market Contribution: Determine if the portfolio underperformed due to a general market downturn.

2. Sector Allocation: Analyze whether an overweight in technology and an underweight in utilities contributed to the deviation.

3. Security Selection: Assess if particular stock choices, like selecting underperforming tech stocks, impacted returns.

4. Currency Effects: Investigate the impact of currency movements, especially if the portfolio includes foreign stocks.

5. Interest Rate Effects: Examine the influence of interest rate changes on any bond holdings within the portfolio.

Dissecting the portfolio's performance through these lenses, you can provide a detailed explanation to stakeholders, adjust your strategies accordingly, and enhance future performance. This analytical rigor not only improves decision-making but also builds credibility and trust with investors.

P&L attribution is a powerful tool in the arsenal of financial analysts and portfolio managers. By leveraging the capabilities of the Pandas library, you can perform detailed, insightful analyses that reveal the underlying drivers of portfolio performance. This not only aids in better decision-making but also enhances accountability and transparency in financial reporting. As you continue to build your expertise, these skills will prove invaluable in navigating the complexities of financial markets.

Risk-Adjusted Return Measures

Key Risk-Adjusted Return Metrics

1. Sharpe Ratio

The Sharpe Ratio, developed by Nobel laureate William F. Sharpe, is one of the most widely used risk-adjusted return measures. It evaluates the excess return per unit of risk (standard deviation) and is calculated as follows:

$$
Sharpe\ Ratio = \frac{R_p - R_f}{\sigma_p}
$$

- R_p: Portfolio return
- R_f: Risk-free rate
- σ_p: Standard deviation of portfolio return

This ratio helps in understanding whether the returns are due to smart investment decisions or excessive risk-taking.

2. Sortino Ratio

The Sortino Ratio is a refinement of the Sharpe Ratio. It differentiates harmful volatility (downside risk) from total overall volatility. The formula is:

$$

Sortino\ Ratio = \frac{R_p - R_f}{\sigma_d}
$$

- \(\sigma_d\): Standard deviation of negative asset returns (downside deviation)

This makes the Sortino Ratio particularly useful in evaluating investments with non-normal return distributions.

3. Treynor Ratio

The Treynor Ratio measures returns earned in excess of what could have been earned on a risk-free investment per unit of market risk. It's calculated as:

$$
Treynor\ Ratio = \frac{R_p - R_f}{\beta_p}
$$

- \(\beta_p\): Portfolio beta (measure of sensitivity to market movements)

The Treynor Ratio is suited for evaluating the performance of diversified portfolios where systematic risk is the primary concern.

4. Jensen's Alpha

Jensen's Alpha measures the excess return generated by a portfolio over the expected return predicted by the Capital Asset Pricing Model (CAPM). It is expressed as:

$$
\alpha = R\_p - [R\_f + \beta\_p (R\_m - R\_f)]
$$

- \(R_m\): Market return

A positive alpha indicates that the portfolio has outperformed the market on a risk-adjusted basis.

Step-by-Step Guide to Calculating Risk-Adjusted Return Measures Using Pandas

1. Data Preparation

Prepare the necessary data, including portfolio returns, risk-free rates, and market returns.

```python
import pandas as pd

# Load portfolio return data
port_returns = pd.read_csv('portfolio_returns.csv',
parse_dates=['Date'], index_col='Date')

# Load risk-free rate data
risk_free_rate = pd.read_csv('risk_free_rate.csv',
parse_dates=['Date'], index_col='Date')

# Load market return data
market_returns = pd.read_csv('market_returns.csv',
```

```python
parse_dates=['Date'], index_col='Date')
```

2. Calculating the Sharpe Ratio

Compute the Sharpe Ratio by calculating the excess return and dividing it by the standard deviation of the portfolio returns.

```python
# Calculate excess returns
excess_returns        =        port_returns['Return']        -
risk_free_rate['RiskFreeRate']

# Calculate the Sharpe Ratio
sharpe_ratio = excess_returns.mean() / excess_returns.std()
print(f'Sharpe Ratio: {sharpe_ratio:.2f}')
```

3. Calculating the Sortino Ratio

Filter negative returns to compute the downside deviation and then calculate the Sortino Ratio.

```python
# Calculate downside deviation
downside_deviation    =    excess_returns[excess_returns    <
0].std()

# Calculate the Sortino Ratio
sortino_ratio = excess_returns.mean() / downside_deviation
```

```python
print(f'Sortino Ratio: {sortino_ratio:.2f}')
```
` ` `

4. Calculating the Treynor Ratio

Estimate the beta of the portfolio by regressing portfolio returns against market returns. Then, use this beta to compute the Treynor Ratio.

` ` `python
```python
import numpy as np
import statsmodels.api as sm

# Regress portfolio returns on market returns to get beta
X = sm.add_constant(market_returns['Return'])
model = sm.OLS(port_returns['Return'], X).fit()
beta = model.params['Return']

# Calculate the Treynor Ratio
treynor_ratio = excess_returns.mean() / beta
print(f'Treynor Ratio: {treynor_ratio:.2f}')
```
` ` `

5. Calculating Jensen's Alpha

Use the CAPM formula to compute Jensen's Alpha.

` ` `python
```python
# Calculate expected portfolio return using CAPM
```

```
expected_port_return     =     risk_free_rate['RiskFreeRate']
+    beta    *    (market_returns['Return'].mean()    -
risk_free_rate['RiskFreeRate'].mean())

# Calculate Jensen's Alpha
jensen_alpha     =     port_returns['Return'].mean()    -
expected_port_return.mean()
print(f'Jensen's Alpha: {jensen_alpha:.2f}')
```
```
```

Practical Application: Case Study

Consider a hedge fund managing a diversified portfolio that spans equities, bonds, and commodities. Over the past year, the fund has achieved a return of 12%, while the market return stood at 10%. The risk-free rate was consistently around 2%. Using the above methodologies, you can calculate the fund's Sharpe Ratio, Sortino Ratio, Treynor Ratio, and Jensen's Alpha to evaluate performance comprehensively.

1. Sharpe Ratio: Determines the efficiency of the fund in balancing risk and return.

2. Sortino Ratio: Highlights the fund's performance in mitigating downside risk, appealing to risk-averse investors.

3. Treynor Ratio: Assesses the returns generated per unit of systematic risk, crucial for understanding market sensitivity.

4. Jensen's Alpha: Offers insight into the fund's ability to generate returns above those predicted by the market model, indicating superior portfolio management skills.

Risk-adjusted return measures are indispensable tools for financial analysts and portfolio managers, providing nuanced insights into the performance of investment strategies. By leveraging the powerful data manipulation capabilities of the Pandas library, you can effectively compute these metrics and make informed, strategic decisions. Mastering these skills not only enhances your analytical capabilities but also positions you as a knowledgeable and effective financial professional in the competitive world of finance.

Hedging Strategies with Pandas

Hedging is not about eliminating risk entirely but about reducing it to a manageable level. For instance, if you hold a portfolio of stocks, you might use options or futures contracts to hedge against a potential decline in stock prices. The primary goal is to offset potential losses in one position by taking an opposing position in another.

Key Hedging Strategies

1. Using Options for Hedging

Options are versatile financial instruments that can provide downside protection while still allowing for upside potential. Key strategies include:

- Protective Puts: Buying a put option on an asset you already own ensures that you can sell it at a predetermined price, thus limiting your losses.
- Covered Calls: Selling a call option on an asset you own generates premium income, which can offset potential losses if the asset's price declines.

2. Futures Contracts

A futures contract is an agreement to buy or sell an asset at a future date for a predetermined price. Futures can be used to hedge against price fluctuations in commodities, currencies, or indexes.

3. Forward Contracts

Similar to futures, forward contracts are customized agreements between two parties to buy or sell an asset at a specified future date and price. They are often used in foreign exchange markets to hedge against currency risk.

4. Diversification

Diversification involves spreading investments across various asset classes, sectors, and geographies to reduce exposure to any single risk. It is a fundamental strategy that can effectively mitigate risk without requiring complex financial instruments.

Implementing Hedging Strategies Using Pandas

1. Data Preparation

Let's start by preparing the necessary data, including asset prices, option data, and futures prices.

```python
import pandas as pd
```

```python
# Load stock price data
stock_prices = pd.read_csv('stock_prices.csv',
parse_dates=['Date'], index_col='Date')

# Load options data
options_data = pd.read_csv('options_data.csv',
parse_dates=['Date'], index_col='Date')

# Load futures data
futures_data = pd.read_csv('futures_data.csv',
parse_dates=['Date'], index_col='Date')
```

2. Protective Put Strategy

To implement a protective put strategy, we'll need to calculate the potential losses and the corresponding protection provided by the put option.

```python
# Assume we own 100 shares of the stock
num_shares = 100

# Calculate potential losses without protection
potential_losses = stock_prices['Close'] - stock_prices['Close'].shift(1)
potential_losses = potential_losses.fillna(0) * num_shares

# Load put option prices
```

```python
put_option_prices = options_data[options_data['Type'] ==
'Put']['Price']

# Calculate protection provided by the put option
put_protection = (put_option_prices -
put_option_prices.shift(1)).fillna(0) * num_shares

# Calculate net position with protective put
net_position = potential_losses + put_protection
```

3. Implementing a Covered Call Strategy

Covered calls involve selling a call option on an asset you own. This generates premium income, which can offset potential losses in the stock.

```python
# Load call option prices
call_option_prices = options_data[options_data['Type'] ==
'Call']['Price']

# Calculate premium income from selling call options
premium_income = call_option_prices * num_shares

# Calculate net position with covered call
net_position_with_covered_call = potential_losses -
premium_income.shift(1).fillna(0)
```

4. Hedging with Futures Contracts

Using futures to hedge involves taking a position opposite to your current holdings. For example, if you hold a long position in a stock, you might enter into a short futures contract to hedge against a decline in the stock's price.

```python
# Load futures prices
futures_prices = futures_data['Price']

# Assume we have a futures contract size of 100 units
futures_contract_size = 100

# Calculate potential gains/losses from futures position
futures_gains_losses = (futures_prices - futures_prices.shift(1)).fillna(0) * futures_contract_size

# Calculate net position with futures hedge
net_position_with_futures_hedge = potential_losses + futures_gains_losses
```

Practical Application: Case Study

Imagine you're managing a portfolio with significant exposure to a volatile stock. To protect your portfolio from potential losses, you decide to implement a protective put strategy. Over a six-month period, the stock market experiences heightened volatility, with significant price swings. By executing the protective put strategy, you manage to cap your losses, demonstrating the effectiveness of options in hedging.

1. Protective Put: By buying put options, you managed to safeguard your portfolio from severe declines, providing peace of mind during turbulent market phases.

2. Covered Call: The premium income from selling call options helped offset minor losses, ensuring a steady cash flow.

3. Futures Contracts: Short futures positions counterbalanced the long stock positions, illustrating how futures can effectively hedge against market downturns.

Hedging strategies are indispensable tools for financial professionals, offering a way to manage and mitigate risks. By leveraging the Pandas library, you can seamlessly integrate these strategies into your workflow, providing robust protection for your investment portfolios. Mastering these techniques not only enhances your risk management capabilities but also positions you as a strategic thinker in the world of finance.

Case Study: Risk Management in Practice

Context and Background

Imagine you are the Chief Risk Officer of a mid-sized investment firm based in Vancouver. Your firm manages a diversified portfolio, including equities, bonds, and commodities. Recently, the market has shown increased volatility due to geopolitical uncertainties and shifts in economic policies. Your primary objective is to ensure the portfolio remains resilient against potential market downturns.

Setting the Scene: Initial Risk Assessment

The first step in effective risk management is conducting a thorough risk assessment. Utilizing Pandas, you can analyze historical data to understand the portfolio's exposure to various risk factors.

Data Collection

Begin by gathering historical price data for the assets in your portfolio. This includes equities, bonds, and commodity prices. Additionally, you'll need macroeconomic indicators that might influence these assets, such as interest rates, inflation rates, and economic growth figures.

```python
import pandas as pd

# Load historical price data
equities_data = pd.read_csv('equities_data.csv', parse_dates=['Date'], index_col='Date')
bonds_data = pd.read_csv('bonds_data.csv', parse_dates=['Date'], index_col='Date')
commodities_data = pd.read_csv('commodities_data.csv', parse_dates=['Date'], index_col='Date')

# Load macroeconomic indicators
macro_data = pd.read_csv('macro_data.csv', parse_dates=['Date'], index_col='Date')
```

```
` ` `
```

Initial Analysis: Volatility and Correlation

Next, calculate the historical volatility of each asset and examine the correlations among them. High correlations between assets can indicate higher portfolio risk.

```python
# Calculate daily returns
equities_returns = equities_data.pct_change().dropna()
bonds_returns = bonds_data.pct_change().dropna()
commodities_returns                              =
commodities_data.pct_change().dropna()

# Calculate volatility (standard deviation of returns)
equities_volatility = equities_returns.std()
bonds_volatility = bonds_returns.std()
commodities_volatility = commodities_returns.std()

# Calculate correlation matrix
returns_data = pd.concat([equities_returns, bonds_returns, commodities_returns], axis=1)
correlation_matrix = returns_data.corr()
` ` `
```

Implementing Risk Management Strategies

With an understanding of the portfolio's risk profile, you can now implement various risk management strategies to mitigate potential losses.

Value-at-Risk (VaR) Calculation

VaR is a widely used risk metric that estimates the potential loss in value of a portfolio over a given time period, at a specified confidence level.

```python
import numpy as np

# Define confidence level and time period
confidence_level = 0.95
time_period = 10 # days

# Calculate portfolio returns
portfolio_returns = returns_data.mean(axis=1)

# Calculate VaR using the historical method
VaR = np.percentile(portfolio_returns, (1 - confidence_level) * 100) * np.sqrt(time_period)

print(f'VaR at {confidence_level} confidence level over {time_period} days: {VaR}')
```

Stress Testing

Stress testing involves simulating extreme market conditions to assess the portfolio's resilience. This can be done by applying historical scenarios or hypothetical shocks to the data.

```python
# Define stress scenario: sudden market downturn of 10%
shock_factor = -0.10

# Apply shock to the portfolio
stressed_portfolio_returns = portfolio_returns * (1 + shock_factor)

# Calculate potential losses under stress scenario
stress_test_loss = stressed_portfolio_returns.min()

print(f'Potential loss under stress scenario: {stress_test_loss}')
```

Adjusting the Portfolio: Hedging and Diversification

To mitigate identified risks, you might decide to hedge certain exposures or diversify the portfolio further.

Hedging with Options

Let's say you decide to hedge the equity portion of the portfolio using put options. This involves buying put options, which increase in value as the underlying asset's price declines.

```python
# Load put option prices
put_option_prices = pd.read_csv('put_option_prices.csv',
```

```python
parse_dates=['Date'], index_col='Date')

# Assume we own 1000 shares of the stock
num_shares = 1000

# Calculate protection provided by the put option
put_protection              =              (put_option_prices          -
put_option_prices.shift(1)).fillna(0) * num_shares

# Calculate net position with protective put
equities_losses = equities_returns * num_shares
net_position_with_put = equities_losses + put_protection
```

Diversification Strategy

You can also mitigate risk by diversifying into less correlated assets, such as adding more bonds or commodities to the portfolio.

```python
# Calculate new portfolio allocation
new_allocation = {
    'Equities': 0.4,
    'Bonds': 0.4,
    'Commodities': 0.2
}

# Rebalance portfolio based on new allocation
```

```python
rebalanced_portfolio_returns = (
    equities_returns * new_allocation['Equities'] +
    bonds_returns * new_allocation['Bonds'] +
    commodities_returns * new_allocation['Commodities']
)

# Recalculate portfolio volatility and VaR
new_portfolio_volatility = rebalanced_portfolio_returns.std()
new_VaR = np.percentile(rebalanced_portfolio_returns, (1 - confidence_level) * 100) * np.sqrt(time_period)

print(f'New portfolio volatility: {new_portfolio_volatility}')
print(f'New VaR at {confidence_level} confidence level over {time_period} days: {new_VaR}')
```

Monitoring and Reporting

Risk management is an ongoing process. Regularly monitor the portfolio's risk metrics and adjust strategies as market conditions change. Using Pandas, you can automate daily risk reporting to ensure timely decision-making.

```python
# Generate daily risk report
daily_risk_report = {
    'Date': equities_data.index[-1],
    'Equities Volatility': equities_volatility,
    'Bonds Volatility': bonds_volatility,
```

```
    'Commodities Volatility': commodities_volatility,
    'Portfolio VaR': VaR,
    'Stress Test Loss': stress_test_loss
}

daily_risk_report_df = pd.DataFrame([daily_risk_report])
daily_risk_report_df.to_csv('daily_risk_report.csv',
index=False)
```
```

Through this case study, you have seen how the Pandas library can be a powerful tool in the arsenal of any financial professional dedicated to robust risk management. By leveraging Pandas' capabilities, you can effectively analyze, monitor, and mitigate risks, ensuring your portfolio remains resilient in the face of market uncertainties. Whether through calculating key metrics like VaR, performing stress tests, or implementing hedging strategies, Pandas offers the flexibility and efficiency needed to safeguard your investments. This practical approach to risk management not only enhances financial stability but also positions you as a proactive and strategic leader in the financial industry.
```

CHAPTER 6:
ADVANCED TOPICS
AND REAL-WORLD
APPLICATIONS

Machine learning (ML) offers unparalleled capabilities in pattern recognition, predictive analytics, and data-driven decision-making. With the capacity to process and analyse large volumes of data, ML models can uncover insights that traditional statistical methods might miss. In finance, where timely and accurate predictions can lead to substantial gains or prevent significant losses, ML is invaluable.

Data Preparation: The Foundation of Machine Learning

Before diving into model building, the importance of data preparation cannot be overstated. Clean, well-structured data is the bedrock of any successful machine learning project.

Loading and Exploring Financial Data

Start by loading your financial datasets, which might include historical stock prices, trading volumes, and economic indicators. Use Pandas to import and explore this data.

```python
import pandas as pd

# Load historical stock price data
stock_data = pd.read_csv('historical_stock_prices.csv', parse_dates=['Date'], index_col='Date')

# Display basic information about the dataset
print(stock_data.info())
print(stock_data.head())
```

Observing the structure and content of your data helps identify any inconsistencies or missing values that need addressing.

Data Cleaning and Feature Engineering

Clean the data by handling missing values and outliers. Additionally, create new features that might enhance the predictive power of your models, such as moving averages or momentum indicators.

```python
# Fill missing values using forward fill method
stock_data.fillna(method='ffill', inplace=True)
```

```python
# Create moving average features
stock_data['MA_20']                                    =
stock_data['Close'].rolling(window=20).mean()
stock_data['MA_50']                                    =
stock_data['Close'].rolling(window=50).mean()

# Create momentum indicator
stock_data['Momentum']        =        stock_data['Close']        -
stock_data['Close'].shift(5)

# Drop rows with NaN values after feature creation
stock_data.dropna(inplace=True)
```

Building Predictive Models

With clean and enriched data, proceed to model building. Here, we'll explore different machine learning algorithms and their application in financial predictions.

Linear Regression: A Simple Yet Powerful Tool

Linear regression is a fundamental predictive modelling technique that can be a good starting point. It aims to model the relationship between a dependent variable and one or more independent variables.

```python
from sklearn.model_selection import train_test_split
from sklearn.linear_model import LinearRegression
```

```
from sklearn.metrics import mean_squared_error

# Define target variable (Close price) and feature set
X = stock_data[['MA_20', 'MA_50', 'Momentum']]
y = stock_data['Close']

# Split the dataset into training and testing sets
X_train, X_test, y_train, y_test = train_test_split(X, y,
test_size=0.2, random_state=42)

# Initialize and train the linear regression model
lr_model = LinearRegression()
lr_model.fit(X_train, y_train)

# Make predictions
y_pred = lr_model.predict(X_test)

# Evaluate the model
mse = mean_squared_error(y_test, y_pred)
print(f'Mean Squared Error: {mse}')
```

While linear regression is straightforward, it may not capture complex patterns in financial data. This is where more advanced algorithms come into play.

Random Forest: Robust and Versatile

Random Forests, an ensemble learning method, can handle large datasets with higher dimensionality and complex interactions between features.

```python
from sklearn.ensemble import RandomForestRegressor

# Initialize and train the random forest model
rf_model    =    RandomForestRegressor(n_estimators=100,
random_state=42)
rf_model.fit(X_train, y_train)

# Make predictions
y_pred_rf = rf_model.predict(X_test)

# Evaluate the model
mse_rf = mean_squared_error(y_test, y_pred_rf)
print(f'Mean Squared Error (Random Forest): {mse_rf}')
```

Random Forests often outperform simpler models by reducing overfitting and capturing more intricate relationships in the data.

Neural Networks: Capturing Deep Patterns

For even more complex datasets, neural networks can be highly effective. These models, inspired by the human brain, are capable of learning deep, non-linear relationships.

```python
from keras.models import Sequential
```

```python
from keras.layers import Dense

# Define the neural network architecture
model = Sequential()
model.add(Dense(units=64,                    activation='relu',
input_shape=(X_train.shape[1],)))
model.add(Dense(units=32, activation='relu'))
model.add(Dense(units=1))

# Compile and train the model
model.compile(optimizer='adam', loss='mean_squared_error')
model.fit(X_train,    y_train,    epochs=50,    batch_size=10,
validation_split=0.2)

# Make predictions
y_pred_nn = model.predict(X_test)

# Evaluate the model
mse_nn = mean_squared_error(y_test, y_pred_nn)
print(f'Mean Squared Error (Neural Network): {mse_nn}')
```
```

Neural networks can capture highly complex patterns, making them suitable for sophisticated financial predictions.

Model Evaluation and Validation

Evaluating the performance of machine learning models is crucial to ensure their accuracy and reliability. Use metrics like Mean Squared Error (MSE), Mean Absolute Error (MAE), and R-
```

squared to assess performance.

```python
from sklearn.metrics import mean_absolute_error, r2_score

# Calculate additional evaluation metrics
mae = mean_absolute_error(y_test, y_pred)
r2 = r2_score(y_test, y_pred)

print(f'Mean Absolute Error: {mae}')
print(f'R-squared: {r2}')
```

Additionally, consider cross-validation techniques to ensure that the model's performance is consistent across different subsets of the data.

```python
from sklearn.model_selection import cross_val_score

# Perform cross-validation
cv_scores = cross_val_score(lr_model, X, y, cv=5, scoring='neg_mean_squared_error')
cv_mse = -cv_scores.mean()

print(f'Cross-validated Mean Squared Error: {cv_mse}')
```

Practical Applications and Case Studies

To illustrate the power of machine learning in financial predictions, let's explore a practical case study: predicting stock prices for a major technology company.

Case Study: Predicting Stock Prices of a Major Tech Company

In this case study, we'll use historical data and machine learning algorithms to predict the future prices of a well-known technology company's stock.

1. Data Collection: Gather historical stock prices and relevant economic indicators.

2. Feature Engineering: Create features that capture market trends, such as moving averages, trading volume, and momentum indicators.

3. Model Selection: Choose and train multiple machine learning models, including linear regression, random forests, and neural networks.

4. Model Evaluation: Assess the models' performance using appropriate metrics and select the best-performing model.

5. Prediction and Analysis: Use the chosen model to predict future stock prices and analyze the results.

```python
# Assume feature engineering and model training have been completed as shown above

# Predict future stock prices
future_dates = pd.date_range(start='2023-01-01', end='2023-12-31')

future_features = create_features(future_dates) # Function to
```

create features for future dates

```
# Make predictions using the best-performing model (e.g.,
Random Forest)
future_predictions = rf_model.predict(future_features)

# Plot the predictions
import matplotlib.pyplot as plt

plt.figure(figsize=(12, 6))
plt.plot(future_dates, future_predictions, label='Predicted
Prices')
plt.title('Predicted Stock Prices for 2023')
plt.xlabel('Date')
plt.ylabel('Price')
plt.legend()
plt.show()
```
` ` `

Through this case study, you see how machine learning can provide actionable insights and enhance decision-making in financial markets.

Understanding Sentiment Analysis in Finance

Sentiment analysis, also known as opinion mining, involves extracting subjective information from textual data. In the financial context, sentiment analysis aims to determine the general mood or tone of news articles, social media posts, and other textual sources about financial instruments, companies, or markets. By analyzing these sentiments, traders and analysts can predict market movements, identify trends, and make informed investment decisions.

Data Collection: Harvesting Financial News

The first step in sentiment analysis is gathering relevant data. Financial news can be sourced from various online platforms, including news websites, financial blogs, and social media channels. For this example, let's use web scraping techniques to collect news articles.

```python
import requests
from bs4 import BeautifulSoup

# Function to scrape financial news from a website
def scrape_news(url):
    response = requests.get(url)
    soup = BeautifulSoup(response.text, 'html.parser')

    # Extract news headlines
    headlines = [item.text for item in soup.find_all('h2',
class_='headline')]
    return headlines

# Example URL
news_url = 'https://www.financialnewswebsite.com'
financial_news = scrape_news(news_url)

# Display some of the scraped headlines
```

```python
print(financial_news[:5])
```
` ` `

This basic web scraping code provides a starting point for collecting financial news headlines. For more comprehensive scraping, you may need to navigate through pagination, extract article bodies, and handle various HTML structures.

Data Cleaning and Preprocessing: Preparing Text for Analysis

Once the news data is collected, it needs to be cleaned and preprocessed. Text data often contains noise, such as HTML tags, punctuation, and stopwords, which must be removed to facilitate effective analysis.

```python
import re
import nltk
from nltk.corpus import stopwords

# Download stopwords
nltk.download('stopwords')

# Function to clean and preprocess text
def preprocess_text(text):
    # Remove HTML tags
    text = re.sub(r'<.*?>', '', text)

    # Remove punctuation and numbers
    text = re.sub(r'[^a-zA-Z]', ' ', text)
```

```python
    # Convert to lower case
    text = text.lower()

    # Remove stopwords
    stop_words = set(stopwords.words('english'))
    text = ' '.join([word for word in text.split() if word not in stop_words])

    return text

# Apply preprocessing to each headline
cleaned_news = [preprocess_text(headline) for headline in financial_news]

# Display some of the cleaned headlines
print(cleaned_news[:5])
```

Preprocessing ensures that the text data is in a consistent and analyzable format, ready for sentiment analysis.

Sentiment Analysis with NLP Libraries

With clean text data, the next step is to perform sentiment analysis. Various NLP libraries, such as TextBlob, VADER (Valence Aware Dictionary and Sentiment Reasoner), and NLTK, can be used for this purpose. In this example, we'll use TextBlob, a simple yet powerful library for NLP tasks.

```python
```

```
from textblob import TextBlob

# Function to analyze sentiment
def analyze_sentiment(text):
    blob = TextBlob(text)
    # TextBlob returns polarity: -1 (negative) to 1 (positive)
    return blob.sentiment.polarity

# Apply sentiment analysis to each cleaned headline
sentiments = [analyze_sentiment(headline) for headline in cleaned_news]

# Combine headlines with their sentiment scores into a DataFrame
news_df = pd.DataFrame({'headline': financial_news, 'sentiment': sentiments})

# Display the DataFrame
print(news_df.head())
```
```

By using TextBlob, we can assign sentiment scores to each news headline, quantifying the overall sentiment in our dataset.

Visualizing Sentiment Trends

Visualizing sentiment data can reveal trends and patterns that inform trading strategies and market analysis. Let's create visualizations to understand the sentiment distribution and its changes over time.
```

```python
import matplotlib.pyplot as plt

# Plot sentiment distribution
plt.figure(figsize=(10, 6))
plt.hist(news_df['sentiment'], bins=20, edgecolor='k')
plt.title('Sentiment Distribution')
plt.xlabel('Sentiment Score')
plt.ylabel('Frequency')
plt.show()

# Assuming we have timestamps for the headlines
news_df['date'] = pd.date_range(start='2023-01-01', periods=len(news_df), freq='D')

# Plot sentiment over time
plt.figure(figsize=(12, 6))
plt.plot(news_df['date'], news_df['sentiment'], marker='o', linestyle='-')
plt.title('Sentiment Over Time')
plt.xlabel('Date')
plt.ylabel('Sentiment Score')
plt.show()
```

These visualizations help identify periods of positive or negative sentiment, providing insights into market psychology and potential trading opportunities.

Case Study: Sentiment Analysis for Stock Market Prediction

To illustrate the practical application of sentiment analysis, let's conduct a case study predicting stock price movements based on sentiment scores from financial news.

Case Study Steps

1. Data Collection: Gather historical stock prices and corresponding news headlines.

2. Sentiment Analysis: Calculate sentiment scores for the news headlines.

3. Feature Engineering: Create sentiment-based features and merge them with stock price data.

4. Model Training: Train machine learning models using the combined dataset.

5. Prediction and Evaluation: Predict stock prices and evaluate model performance.

```python
# Assuming stock_data and news_df are already defined as
shown earlier

# Merge stock data with sentiment scores
stock_data = stock_data.reset_index()

combined_data = pd.merge(stock_data, news_df[['date',
'sentiment']], left_on='Date', right_on='date')

# Drop rows with NaN values
combined_data.dropna(inplace=True)
```

```
# Define target variable (Close price) and feature set including sentiment
X = combined_data[['MA_20', 'MA_50', 'Momentum', 'sentiment']]
y = combined_data['Close']

# Split the dataset into training and testing sets
X_train, X_test, y_train, y_test = train_test_split(X, y, test_size=0.2, random_state=42)

# Initialize and train the random forest model
rf_model = RandomForestRegressor(n_estimators=100, random_state=42)
rf_model.fit(X_train, y_train)

# Make predictions
y_pred_rf = rf_model.predict(X_test)

# Evaluate the model
mse_rf = mean_squared_error(y_test, y_pred_rf)
print(f'Mean Squared Error (Random Forest with Sentiment): {mse_rf}')
```
```

Incorporating sentiment analysis into our predictive models, we can capture the influence of market sentiment on stock prices, potentially improving forecast accuracy.
```

Algorithmic Trading with Pandas

Introduction to Algorithmic Trading

Algorithmic trading, often referred to as algo-trading or automated trading, involves the use of computer algorithms to manage the buying and selling of financial instruments. These algorithms can execute trades based on a predefined set of rules and conditions, covering various strategies such as market making, arbitrage, and trend following.

To get started with algorithmic trading using Pandas, we need to understand how to process, analyze, and manipulate large datasets efficiently. Pandas provides a robust framework for these tasks, offering powerful data structures and functions that simplify complex operations.

Setting Up Your Environment

Before diving into algorithmic trading strategies, ensure you have the necessary libraries installed:

```bash
pip install pandas numpy matplotlib yfinance
```

We'll use Pandas for data manipulation, NumPy for numerical operations, Matplotlib for visualization, and Yahoo Finance (yfinance) to fetch financial data.

Fetching Financial Data

To develop and backtest algorithmic trading strategies, we need historical financial data. The yfinance library offers a convenient way to access this data.

```python
import yfinance as yf
import pandas as pd

# Fetch historical data for a specific stock
symbol = 'AAPL'
data = yf.download(symbol, start='2020-01-01', end='2022-01-01')
data.reset_index(inplace=True)

# Display the first few rows of the data
print(data.head())
```

This code retrieves historical data for Apple Inc. (AAPL) and resets the index to include the Date column.

Developing a Simple Moving Average Crossover Strategy

One popular algorithmic trading strategy is the Simple Moving Average (SMcrossover. This strategy uses two SMAs—a short-term and a long-term average—to generate buy and sell signals. When the short-term SMA crosses above the long-term SMA, it signals a buy; when it crosses below, it signals a sell.

```python
# Calculate short-term and long-term SMAs
data['SMA_20'] = data['Close'].rolling(window=20).mean()
data['SMA_50'] = data['Close'].rolling(window=50).mean()

# Generate buy/sell signals
data['Signal'] = 0
data['Signal'][20:]    =    np.where(data['SMA_20'][20:]    >
data['SMA_50'][20:], 1, -1)
data['Position'] = data['Signal'].diff()

# Display the first few rows with signals
print(data[['Date', 'Close', 'SMA_20', 'SMA_50', 'Signal',
'Position']].head(60))
```

This snippet calculates the 20-day and 50-day SMAs, generates buy/sell signals, and tracks changes in position.

Backtesting the Strategy

Backtesting involves evaluating the performance of a trading strategy using historical data. It helps determine the strategy's effectiveness before deploying it in live trading.

```python
# Initial capital
initial_capital = 100000.0
```

```
# Create a DataFrame to track portfolio value
portfolio = pd.DataFrame(index=data.index)
portfolio['Close'] = data['Close']
portfolio['Signal'] = data['Signal']

# Determine the number of shares to buy/sell
portfolio['Shares'] = initial_capital // data['Close']
portfolio['Holdings'] = portfolio['Shares'] * data['Close']

# Calculate cash and total portfolio value
portfolio['Cash'] = initial_capital - (portfolio['Shares'] * data['Close']).cumsum()
portfolio['Total'] = portfolio['Holdings'] + portfolio['Cash']

# Calculate returns
portfolio['Returns'] = portfolio['Total'].pct_change()

# Display the portfolio's performance
print(portfolio[['Close', 'Holdings', 'Cash', 'Total', 'Returns']].head())
```

This code simulates the buying and selling of shares based on our SMA crossover signals and maintains a record of portfolio performance.

Evaluating Performance Metrics

To evaluate the strategy, we need to analyze performance

metrics such as cumulative returns, drawdown, and Sharpe ratio.

```python
# Calculate cumulative returns
portfolio['Cumulative Returns'] = (1 + portfolio['Returns']).cumprod()

# Calculate drawdown
portfolio['Cumulative Max'] = portfolio['Cumulative Returns'].cummax()
portfolio['Drawdown'] = portfolio['Cumulative Max'] - portfolio['Cumulative Returns']

# Calculate Sharpe ratio
sharpe_ratio = portfolio['Returns'].mean() / portfolio['Returns'].std() * np.sqrt(252)

# Display performance metrics
print(f'Cumulative Returns: {portfolio["Cumulative Returns"].iloc[-1]}')
print(f'Max Drawdown: {portfolio["Drawdown"].max()}')
print(f'Sharpe Ratio: {sharpe_ratio}')
```

These metrics provide insights into the strategy's overall performance, risk, and return characteristics.

Advanced Algorithmic Trading Strategies

Beyond simple strategies, advanced algorithmic trading involves more sophisticated techniques such as machine learning models, sentiment analysis, and high-frequency trading (HFT). Here, we briefly touch on these advanced strategies.

Machine Learning Models

Machine learning models can predict future price movements based on historical data and various indicators. Techniques such as regression, classification, and reinforcement learning are commonly used in this domain.

Sentiment Analysis

Sentiment analysis of news and social media can complement traditional trading signals. By analyzing the sentiment of financial news, traders can gauge market sentiment and adjust their strategies accordingly.

High-Frequency Trading

HFT involves executing a large number of orders at extremely high speeds. It requires low-latency data feeds and advanced infrastructure to capitalize on minute market inefficiencies.

Algorithmic trading with Pandas opens the door to sophisticated trading strategies that can be backtested and refined with ease. By leveraging the powerful data manipulation capabilities of Pandas alongside other libraries, you can develop, evaluate, and optimize trading algorithms that enhance your financial decision-making. As you delve deeper into algorithmic trading, you'll discover a wealth of opportunities to harness technology and data for competitive advantage in the financial markets.

High-Frequency Trading Data Analysis

Understanding High-Frequency Trading Data

High-frequency trading data is characterized by its immense volume and granularity. Unlike traditional datasets, which may record trades on a daily or even minute-by-minute basis, HFT data captures each tick — every individual trade — along with corresponding bid and ask prices, timestamps down to the millisecond, and various other market indicators. This level of detail requires robust data handling and efficient processing methodologies.

```python
import pandas as pd

# Example: Reading high-frequency trading data
file_path = 'path/to/hft_data.csv'
hft_data = pd.read_csv(file_path, parse_dates=['timestamp'])
hft_data.head()
```

Time-Based Indexing and Resampling

Given the importance of time in HFT, precise time-based indexing is crucial. Pandas offers powerful tools for this purpose, allowing us to resample data to different time intervals, such as milliseconds, seconds, or minutes, depending on the analytical requirements.

```python
# Setting the timestamp as the index
hft_data.set_index('timestamp', inplace=True)

# Resampling to 1-second intervals
resampled_data = hft_data.resample('1S').agg({
    'price': 'ohlc', # Open, High, Low, Close
    'volume': 'sum'
})
resampled_data.head()
```

Analyzing Trade Volume and Price Movements

Trade volume and price movements are pivotal in detecting patterns and anomalies in HFT. By aggregating data over specified intervals, we can gain insights into the behavior of market participants, such as identifying sudden spikes in volume or unusual price fluctuations.

```python
# Calculating moving averages
hft_data['price'] = hft_data['price'].astype(float)
```

```python
hft_data['moving_average_5ms']                           =
hft_data['price'].rolling('5ms').mean()

hft_data['moving_average_10ms']                          =
hft_data['price'].rolling('10ms').mean()

# Visualizing price movements
import matplotlib.pyplot as plt

plt.figure(figsize=(10, 6))
plt.plot(hft_data.index, hft_data['price'], label='Price')
plt.plot(hft_data.index,        hft_data['moving_average_5ms'],
label='5ms MA')
plt.plot(hft_data.index,        hft_data['moving_average_10ms'],
label='10ms MA')
plt.legend()
plt.show()
```
```

## Detecting and Handling Outliers

Outliers can significantly skew your analysis and, in high-frequency trading, they can often indicate market anomalies or data errors. Pandas provides functionality to detect and handle these outliers, ensuring the integrity of your analysis.

```python
# Detecting outliers using Z-score
hft_data['price_zscore']        =        (hft_data['price']      -
hft_data['price'].mean()) / hft_data['price'].std()
outliers = hft_data[hft_data['price_zscore'].abs() > 3]
```
```

```
# Handling outliers by capping
hft_data['price']                                        =
hft_data['price'].clip(lower=hft_data['price'].quantile(0.01),
                          upper=hft_data['price'].quantile
(0.99))
```
` ` `

Correlation Analysis

Understanding the correlation between different financial instruments or market indicators can provide insights into trading strategies. Pandas' correlation methods enable you to quantify these relationships effectively.

` ` `python
```
# Example: Calculating correlation matrix
correlation_matrix    =    hft_data[['price',    'volume',
'moving_average_5ms']].corr()
print(correlation_matrix)
```
` ` `

Case Study: Analyzing a Sudden Market Movement

To illustrate the above concepts, let's analyze a case where a sudden market movement occurred. We will investigate the volume spikes and price changes, and visualize how these metrics behaved during the event.

Step 1: Identifying the Event

```python
# Filtering data around the event timestamp
event_start = '2023-01-01 12:00:00.000'
event_end = '2023-01-01 12:01:00.000'
event_data = hft_data[event_start:event_end]
```

Step 2: Visualizing Volume and Price Changes

```python
# Plotting the event data
plt.figure(figsize=(10, 6))
plt.plot(event_data.index, event_data['price'], label='Price')
plt.bar(event_data.index, event_data['volume'], alpha=0.3, label='Volume')
plt.legend()
plt.title('Volume and Price Changes During Market Event')
plt.show()
```

Step 3: Analyzing Market Reactions

```python
# Calculating post-event metrics
post_event_start = '2023-01-01 12:01:00.000'
post_event_end = '2023-01-01 12:02:00.000'
post_event_data = hft_data[post_event_start:post_event_end]
```

```
# Metrics such as average price and volume
average_price_post_event = post_event_data['price'].mean()
average_volume_post_event                    =
post_event_data['volume'].mean()

print(f"Average Price Post Event: {average_price_post_event}")
print(f"Average         Volume         Post         Event:
{average_volume_post_event}")
```
```

Following these steps, analysts can dissect high-frequency trading data to uncover critical insights, guiding strategic decision-making in the fast-paced financial markets. This comprehensive approach using Pandas equips professionals with the tools to handle and interpret the complexities of HFT, driving efficiency and precision in their analyses.

## Quantitative Finance and Model Implementation

Quantitative finance leverages a blend of mathematical rigor, computer science, and financial theory. The goal is to develop models that can predict market behaviour, optimize portfolios, and manage financial risks. These models often require the processing and analysis of large datasets, making Pandas an invaluable tool for quant practitioners.

## Preparing Financial Data for Modeling

Before diving into model implementation, it's crucial to ensure that your data is clean, structured, and ready for analysis. This involves importing financial data, handling missing values,
```

and performing exploratory data analysis (EDto understand the underlying patterns and distributions.

```python
import pandas as pd

# Example: Reading financial data
file_path = 'path/to/financial_data.csv'
financial_data = pd.read_csv(file_path, parse_dates=['date'])
financial_data.set_index('date', inplace=True)
financial_data.head()

# Handling missing values
financial_data.fillna(method='ffill', inplace=True)

# Descriptive statistics
financial_data.describe()
```

Implementing a Simple Linear Regression Model

Linear regression is a foundational model in quantitative finance, used to predict the relationship between a dependent variable (e.g., stock price) and one or more independent variables (e.g., market indices, interest rates). Using Pandas alongside libraries like Statsmodels, we can easily implement and interpret linear regression models.

```python
import statsmodels.api as sm
```

```python
# Define dependent and independent variables
X = financial_data[['market_index', 'interest_rate']]
y = financial_data['stock_price']

# Add a constant to the model
X = sm.add_constant(X)

# Fit the linear regression model
model = sm.OLS(y, X).fit()

# Model summary
print(model.summary())
```

Time Series Analysis and Autoregressive Models

Time series analysis is pivotal in quantitative finance for modeling and forecasting financial data. One common approach is using Autoregressive Integrated Moving Average (ARIMmodels, which combine autoregression and moving averages to capture the temporal dependencies in the data.

```python
from statsmodels.tsa.arima.model import ARIMA

# Fit an ARIMA model
order = (5, 1, 0)  # (p, d, q)
arima_model     =     ARIMA(financial_data['stock_price'],
order=order)
```

```python
arima_result = arima_model.fit()

# Summary of the model
print(arima_result.summary())

# Forecasting
forecast = arima_result.forecast(steps=10)
print(forecast)
```

Portfolio Optimization with Mean-Variance Analysis

Modern portfolio theory (MPT) is a cornerstone of quantitative finance, focusing on the optimization of investment portfolios by balancing risk and return. Using Pandas, we can implement mean-variance optimization to determine the optimal asset allocation.

```python
import numpy as np

# Calculate daily returns
returns = financial_data.pct_change().dropna()

# Calculate mean returns and covariance matrix
mean_returns = returns.mean()
cov_matrix = returns.cov()

# Define portfolio weights
num_assets = len(mean_returns)
```

```python
weights = np.random.random(num_assets)
weights /= np.sum(weights)

# Calculate portfolio return and risk
portfolio_return = np.sum(weights * mean_returns)
portfolio_risk = np.sqrt(np.dot(weights.T, np.dot(cov_matrix, weights)))

print(f"Portfolio Return: {portfolio_return}")
print(f"Portfolio Risk: {portfolio_risk}")
```

Implementing Risk Management Models

Effective risk management is vital in quantitative finance. Value-at-Risk (VaR) is a widely used model to quantify potential losses in a portfolio. We can implement VaR using historical simulation, parametric methods, or Monte Carlo simulations.

```python
# Historical Simulation VaR
confidence_level = 0.95
var = np.percentile(returns['stock_price'], (1 - confidence_level) * 100)
print(f"Value-at-Risk (VaR): {var}")

# Parametric VaR
mean_return = returns['stock_price'].mean()
std_dev = returns['stock_price'].std()
```

```python
parametric_var = mean_return + std_dev * np.sqrt(1 - confidence_level)
print(f"Parametric VaR: {parametric_var}")

# Monte Carlo Simulation VaR
simulations = 1000
simulated_returns = np.random.normal(mean_return, std_dev, simulations)
monte_carlo_var = np.percentile(simulated_returns, (1 - confidence_level) * 100)
print(f"Monte Carlo VaR: {monte_carlo_var}")
```

Case Study: Developing a Quantitative Trading Strategy

To bring these concepts together, let's walk through a case study of developing a quantitative trading strategy based on momentum. Momentum strategies exploit the tendency of securities to continue moving in the same direction for some time.

Step 1: Calculate Momentum Indicators

```python
# Calculate moving averages
financial_data['short_window'] = financial_data['stock_price'].rolling(window=40).mean()
financial_data['long_window'] = financial_data['stock_price'].rolling(window=100).mean()

# Generate signals
```

```python
financial_data['signal'] = 0.0

financial_data['signal'][40:]                                    =
np.where(financial_data['short_window'][40:]                     >
financial_data['long_window'][40:], 1.0, 0.0)

financial_data['positions'] = financial_data['signal'].diff()
```

Step 2: Backtesting the Strategy

```python
# Calculate daily returns
financial_data['daily_return']                                   =
financial_data['stock_price'].pct_change()

# Calculate strategy returns
financial_data['strategy_return']                                =
financial_data['signal'].shift(1) * financial_data['daily_return']

# Plot the cumulative returns
financial_data[['daily_return',
'strategy_return']].cumsum().plot()
```

Step 3: Evaluating Performance

```python
# Calculate cumulative returns
cumulative_returns       =       financial_data[['daily_return',
'strategy_return']].cumsum()
```

```
# Performance metrics

sharpe_ratio = financial_data['strategy_return'].mean() / financial_data['strategy_return'].std() * np.sqrt(252)

print(f"Cumulative Returns: {cumulative_returns}")
print(f"Sharpe Ratio: {sharpe_ratio}")
```
```

Implementing these models and techniques, you can develop sophisticated quantitative trading strategies, optimize portfolios, and manage financial risks with precision. The Pandas library, combined with other Python tools, enables you to transform vast amounts of financial data into actionable insights, driving informed decision-making and strategic advantage in the competitive world of finance.
```